walking the small group

TIGHTROPE

Other Books by Bill Donahue and Russ Robinson

Building a Church of Small Groups
Leading Life-Changing Small Groups
The Seven Deadly Sins of Small Group Ministry

Praise for *Walking the Small Group Tightrope*

"Russ Robinson and Bill Donahue brilliantly navigate a legion of complex matters that often steal the transformative power of a group. They are experts and they've made colossal mistakes. They are both humble enough and bold enough to offer us the heartache of their failures and the glory of their Spirit-inspired courage. This book will be a standard for all who are serious about seeing God at work in community."

Dan B. Allender Ph.D.
President, Mars Hill Graduate School
author, *The Wounded Heart* and *How Children Raise Parents*

Bill DONAHUE Russ ROBINSON

meeting the challenges
every group faces

walking the small group TIGHTROPE

ZONDERVAN™

Walking the Small Group Tightrope

Requests for information should be addressed to:

Zondervan, *Grand Rapids, Michigan 49530*

Library of Congress Cataloging-in-Publication Data

Donahue, Bill.
Walking the small group tightrope : meeting the challenges every small group faces / Bill Donahue and Russ Robinson.
p. cm.
Includes bibliographical references.
ISBN 0-310-25229-6
1. Church group work. 2. Small groups—Religious aspects—Christianity. 3. Willow Creek Community Church (South Barrington, Ill.) I. Robinson, Russ. II. Title.
BV652.2.D659 2003
253'.7—dc21

2003012689

Interior design by Tracey Moran

Printed in the United States of America

---

10 11 12 13 14 15 . 25 24 23 22 21 20 19 18 17 16 15 14 13 12

contents

acknowledgments

A prevailing church that makes community-building central can truly become a place where nobody stands alone. Such a church has moved from vision — the cosmic ideal of being baptized into one body — to reality, in which community is no longer considered optional.

Writing is similar. Nobody writes alone. And by that we don't just mean we have coauthored some books together. We mean that lots of players have helped us all along the way. We're grateful for the community which has been involved in our writing process.

First and foremost, and especially for this book, we owe an unspeakable debt to Willow Creek's small-group leaders and coaches. You are the ones who have walked the small group tightrope again and again for the past couple of decades, and our learning together has resulted largely from your faithful commitment to serve. Willow's staff keeps pressing us into the rich learning available in this wonderful laboratory we have worked in every day.

So many churches now have a heart for building community, and we have been able to learn from those that have allowed us to come alongside them. One such church is Russ's new church family, Meadowbrook. We wish we could name all the other churches we have learned from. Your willingness to implement emerging ideas keeps informing us all.

ACKNOWLEDGMENTS

We always owe a huge debt to the Willow Creek Association partners involved with us in our ministry and writing. Without Joan Oboyski, we'd rarely get a project off the ground. Christine Anderson, Doug Yonamine, Maryann Whitney, Joe Sherman, and others on the WCA publishing, conferences, marketing, and training teams make our work a joy.

Joan Huyser-Honig gives our work one voice and has made us far better at writing about our ideas than we ever thought we'd be. She and the Zondervan team — including Jack Kuhatschek, Jamie Hinojosa, Alicia Mey, and Brian Phipps — have made our experiences at Willow and elsewhere translate into the real world of small-group life.

We are amazed at the ability of our kids — Ryan and Kinsley (Bill's), and Phil, Mark, and Tim (Russ's) — not only to understand what it is we do but to get excited about it, more than anything because they see in their own lives how small groups have contributed to their growth. And since we have spent many years leading groups with our wives, some of the ideas you'll read about emerged as much from Gail and Lynn as they did from us. When partners for life become partners for ministry, it makes the work we do all the more gratifying.

So we are grateful to so many on whose shoulders we get to stand and proclaim a message we all believe in and love. Thanks . . . for everything.

some problems can't be solved

AN INTRODUCTION TO POLARITY MANAGEMENT

We have been leading or participating in small groups for a combined total of over fifty years. Wow! That makes us feel old, especially with a certain "magic birthday" looming on the horizon for both of us. The two of us have accumulated enough time in the small group leader saddle that you might think we would have figured it all out by now.

Guess again.

Don't get us wrong. We have definitely had our share of small group highs. Some of them even happened when we were leading! But our past is checkered with a considerable number of small group lows.

Good Agendas Gone Bad

I (Bill) remember taking a couples' group on an overnight retreat to spend some focused time on our marriages. It was the ideal setting—a beautiful lake, a private home with water toys and rafts, and two full days together, building community amidst God's glorious creation. There was only one small problem — one very small, whining, crying, screaming, burping problem. The kind with a built-in alarm that goes off at 2 A.M. . . . and 3 A.M. . . . and 4 A.M. The kind of problem that challenges everyone's sanctification. Against my better judgment, I had allowed one couple to bring little Johnny along. After the first night, I found myself wanting to write a children's book called *How to Help Little Johnny Sleep through the Night (and 99 Other Uses for Duct Tape).*

When we tried to gather as a group, it was clear that Johnny's parents were exhausted, group members were annoyed, and the atmosphere was becoming tumultuous. But that didn't stop me from pushing ahead with my agenda. *After all, what's more important — the people or the agenda?*

Using my extensive powers of observation, I asked, "So how's everyone doing? Have you been able to spend some quality time relaxing and talking about your marriage relationships?" Eight sets of eyes focused on me like a foray of heat-seeking missiles. (I couldn't see the ninth set, because my wife was sitting next to me.) Nervous from the response, I unwisely asked a follow-up question. "Scott and Janet, you have been working on your communication together. Uh, how's that going?" Looking back, I should have suggested we all watch a video.

Janet began to cry, while Scott sat motionless and avoided all eye contact. It was painfully uncomfortable and awkward. A perceptive leader would have seen it coming, recognizing not only the couple's tension but also the group's discomfort. Instead of offering friendship and compassion, I provided accountability and called people to accomplish "the mission at hand." Thankfully, by God's grace and with kind input from a few members, we salvaged the weekend and created some memorable moments. But my inability to read the group in that moment almost compromised the community we'd been trying to build together.

I (Russ) misplayed a hand I was dealt just a few years ago in a couples' group Lynn and I were leading. The timing was ironic; I had just been invited to become Willow Creek's director of small groups, a position that would have me eventually guiding a ministry with over 3,500 small group leaders and staff! You would think I wouldn't goof up commonsense relationship dynamics at this stage of my leadership. But I did.

One of the couples in our group started having "marital challenges," a euphemism we use to disguise the relational crisis at hand and pretend it is not serious. We knew danger was lurking around the next bend but tried to ignore it at first. Before long, the couple's marital frustrations began to seep through routine answers to discussion questions, and it was clear they needed help. As they periodically sought our counsel, Lynn and I tried to help them lessen some symptoms of their problems but remained somewhat ignorant and too busy to see the issues for what they really were.

As more of the couple's relational toxins spilled into our group's meetings, we worried about saying anything to the group, fearing it would violate the couple's confidence. But our silence was like throwing a blanket over the proverbial elephant in the room, thinking no one would notice. Unfortunately, this elephant was gaining weight—and fast! Our conclusion? We decided to confront the couple about how their interpersonal conflict was ruining the entire group dynamic.

Well, you can imagine the ensuing train wreck. They were devastated and lashed back with feelings of disappointment and betrayal. In their view, we had responded in glib and superficial ways to their problems and had failed to show them earlier how their behavior was impacting the group. They felt exposed, wounded, and devalued.

Of course, being the spiritual giants we are, we became defensive. We pointed out their unwillingness to seek professional help and insisted they keep their marital problems to themselves during group discussions, unless they were willing to bring the whole sorry tale before the entire group.

(I'm so embarrassed as I write this. What were we thinking?)

Group momentum and growth deteriorated considerably in the coming months, and what had begun as a dream of deeper community turned out to be a nightmare for our group. When the group finally ended, we were drained but relieved. We never really resolved our leadership miscues until many months later. We are grateful that treasured friendships were reconciled, mostly through the grace of couples who chose to focus on what good we did provide them.

But this experience was a confidence rattler for Lynn and me. We thought we had done all the things good small group leaders do. Our review confirmed that most of our moves were by the book. We'd received solid training that helped us foster much good in that little community. But it had all gotten off the rails so easily and quickly. Perhaps we had overlooked something.

"All Learning Comes from Failed Experience"

Despite many successful group experiences filled with rich community and spiritual transformation, some group failures stumped us. From time to time we'd swap personal stories as well as those of other groups that had hit a wall. And we'd wonder if there were common sticking points or mistakes that could be avoided, thus helping groups move forward.

Neither of us wanted to admit what we knew was true. *It wasn't supposed to happen this way! Why did some groups have a wonderful, life-changing experience while others seemed to wander, drift, or just blow up?*

These thoughts were especially troubling for us because we had read so many small group resources and had availed ourselves of loads of training. Our leadership roles have afforded us the opportunity to sit among the best and the brightest when it comes to community building, personal transformation, and group life. And we have grown and changed as a result. But we knew we were still missing some pieces of the puzzle.

Our failures paved the way for fresh insights into how churches and small groups provide members with a transformational experience in community. An unexpected twist revealed our failures as opportunities to learn.

Our leadership team attended a seminar on creative learning strategies, and during introductory comments, the trainer posed what seemed a simple dilemma: "When do people learn?" After we'd provided several inadequate solutions, the trainer rescued us with this simple but profound observation: "When they fail. All learning comes from failed experience." When experience fails to match expectations, the dissonance produces the energy for learning, discovery, and change.

Those words became a kind of mantra for us, stimulating fresh thinking and moving our focus from how badly we had failed to how much we could learn from our failures. This freeing perspective allowed us to realize we had missed some key group dynamics in our understanding and training. It was clear we needed to change how we thought about community life and leadership.

The basic leadership training program we had created was good. Clarity on the fundamentals of small group leadership still mattered. So we remained committed to the tools and training materials we had developed, many of them contained in *Leading Life-Changing Small Groups.*[1] But we knew we were ready to learn more. Thankfully, that learning also came from an unexpected source.

The "Aha" Moment

I (Russ) was having lunch at Willow Creek one day with Wayne Alguire, former Levi Strauss executive and then Willow Creek Association staff member. (Wayne is now the lead pastor of one of Willow's new regional campus sites). Since I was an attorney, and he a corporate executive, our work with Willow sometimes involved legal matters and organizational concerns of the church and Willow Creek Association. Wayne is a voracious reader, so I asked what he'd been reading.

"I'm rereading a favorite from my Levi Strauss days called *Polarity Management,* by Barry Johnson," he remarked.[2] He went on to explain how this book had helped him solve some business problems. For example, how can a business make customers happy and yet produce a profit? Or are these challenges mutually exclusive? Do leaders have to choose between making money and customer satisfaction? Are we here to please shareholders or customers?

In today's business environment, as many of you know, there is no choice; both must be accomplished, or you are out of business. In fact, you have to *exceed* customer expectations and turn them into raving fans. But along the way, you had better make enough profit to pay generous bonuses, overwhelm your lenders, and thrill shareholders at the annual meeting, or you may wind up refurbishing your resume.

Many businesspeople spend an inordinate amount of time trying to find "the answer" to do both things at once. Johnson suggests that maybe there's no magic solution for doing both in business. Rather, they exist in a dynamic tension that a business owner must manage.

My discussion with Wayne gave me an "aha" moment. I immediately started thinking about how this concept applied to many areas, from parenting to church life to small groups. For example, parents have two main jobs. (Actually, therapists agree that parents have 5,493,671 jobs to do. We are focusing on just two to make a point.)

One job is to create a nurturing environment that enfolds children in a safe, healthy family that sticks together through thick and thin. But parents also have to develop their children so they can eventually leave the nest and enter the world's stark realities. The objective is to achieve this by a reasonable age. (For parents, that's 16; for kids, it's 27.) These two worthy goals — forming a close-knit family and developing competent, independent young adults — appear to contradict each other. If you're a parent, you know the tension you live with, especially as your children age, to both embrace and release them — to hold two good things in tension with one another.

Consider the church. We want to reach lost people — missions and evangelism. But we must also meet believers' needs — care and discipleship. It all sounds so straightforward when Jesus says, "Therefore go and make disciples of all nations, baptizing them in the name of the Father and of the Son and of the Holy Spirit, and teaching them to obey everything I have commanded you" (Matt. 28:19–20). Churches have spent two thousand years trying to figure out how to keep both purposes alive, though they appear to tug against one another.

Churches like ours have made the Great Commission a passion, seeking to turn irreligious people into fully devoted followers of Christ. And we have come to recognize the tensions that arise when you allocate staff energy, church resources, and volunteer efforts to the cause. Churches must decide whether the next dollar in the offering plate will support evangelism or discipleship, be strategically invested in the missions ministry agenda or in the Christian education department. Do we put more resources toward reaching skeptics or building up saints? Yet again, two good things stand in tension with each other.

If you subscribe to polarity management theory, it's okay to say sometimes, "There is no answer to that question."

The principles of polarity management suggest that in every area of life we must learn to manage the tension between two good things rather than choose one thing over another. Business leaders strive to make a profit *and* please customers. Good parents make every effort to build close, interdependent relationships with their kids *and* prepare them to live independently when they are grown. Churches must evangelize *and* disciple. In these situations, choosing one thing over another is not an option; we must do both.

The more you understand this principle and observe the world around you, the more often you will spot the examples of this principle. Not every hard-to-solve problem can be stated in terms of polarity. Sometimes a challenge demands more focused attention, further experimentation, and increased creativity. But often when a problem seems intractable or extensive work results in failure, we are missing the obvious.

Johnson's insights were eye opening, but further reflection made us realize how he has simply creatively described what Scripture has always told us. There are many polarities in the kingdom. Jesus called the Twelve to be with him, so that he could send them out (Mark 3:14). Paul reminds us "there is one body and one Spirit ... one lord, one faith, one baptism; one God and Father of all.... *But to each one of us* grace has been given" (Eph. 4:4–7, italics ours). Paul continues by listing individual gifts and ministries. In fact, each one's uniqueness in Christ is the very thing that eternally binds us interdependently to the body as a whole. A community that deplores individuality produces communism. An individual who ignores community embraces narcissism.

Certainly the greatest tension of all time remains an enigma for theologians of every persuasion: reconciling man's free will and God's absolute sovereignty. So Paul can say, "I have become all things to all men so that by all possible means I might save some" (1 Cor. 9:22). Sounds like Paul thinks the whole salvation enterprise depends on his efforts, tact, and ability to accommodate the culture. And yet, regarding salvation and election, in Romans 9 he emphatically states, "It does not, therefore, depend on man's desire or effort, but on God's mercy" (v. 16). Some churches favor the Paul of 1 Corinthians 9, and others the Paul of Romans 9. Both statements reflect a truth in the kingdom and must be held in a dynamic tension. To favor one leads to complacency in evangelism; to favor the other makes us self-glorifying idolaters.

And that's the fundamental benefit behind polarity management. Instead of looking for right answers and nice little definitions, sometimes it's better to identify and manage the tensions that exist between two desirable truths or outcomes. In fact, Johnson actually calls them "unsolvable problems." Good phrase. Makes us sleep better at night!

After learning more about polarity management, we simplified its principles considerably. (This is a fascinating field of study, but we concluded it would be best to use its concepts in distilled form.) Then we applied our learning to small group life as we continued to lead groups. Finally, we began to teach it to small group leaders at Willow Creek and elsewhere.

Once you recognize the benefits of holding two good things in tension, your future gets a little easier to manage. Instead of fighting the tension, you can use it to your advantage. Managing tension keeps things in balance. A trampoline works because it utilizes gravity and elasticity. One without the other would be disastrous.

Ask any tightrope walker. A nice taut rope, stretched appropriately between two good places—the start and the finish—makes for an exciting act. To loosen the rope at either end renders the task impossible. It is the tension that produces results, and an informed and capable walker learns to manage it to his or her advantage. So much of life is the same. Yes, life really is a circus sometimes, and you get to play the tightrope walker.

No Paint by Numbers

Suddenly we realized that what we had previously classified as failures were unseen and unsolvable problems. As we began to apply more of the polarity concept to small groups, things became clearer.

Much teaching in Christian circles implies that if you simply do A, B, C, and D, you will have an abundant life, or become wealthy, or unlock hidden secrets to incredible living, or master biblical community, or avoid financial ruin, or have a powerful prayer experience, or never get cancer, or have a great small group! The problem? We have had small groups in which we've done A, B, C, and D (and even E, F, and G), and guess what? It wasn't so great a small group. Why? Life happens. People sin. The world is a mess.

And the real kicker was, we'd been in or seen other groups in which leaders fumbled and bumbled around, ignoring B and D and doing C before A, and yet ended up with a better experience than others. Now what's up with that? If you fail on A through G, why don't you automatically end up with a bad small group?

Painting by numbers may help organize your color patterns, but it will not produce a life-giving work of art. And leading a small group is more about art than about painting by numbers.

We discovered that it is still essential to know the basics, just as it is in any field or discipline, whether art, music, or auto repair. Understanding A through G (and maybe Z!) matters, but it isn't an automatic formula for success any more than knowing how to use a hammer makes me a carpenter. Every leader should learn how to give people a sense of belonging, help them wrestle with Scripture, lead a good discussion, create a loving environment, and listen carefully to members' needs. Nothing we say in this book undermines the fundamentals of good shepherding.

But as important as all those things are, we stumbled into a second truth, and it is the core of this book. Small group leadership is not a paint-by-numbers exercise in which you'll get a beautiful picture by simply putting the right color on the right number. It really is more of an art—an acrobatic art, if you will. It is the art of managing the dynamic tensions that constantly exist in the context of every group. Entering into the life of a little community requires its participants be aware of these tensions, too.

Every leader and every member must come to grips with this reality. If you do, it will be the most freeing experience you will have in small group life. Master the fundamentals. But be prepared to manage the real tensions and challenges of everyday community. Very often you'll find there are no right answers to some problems that arise in small groups—just several good values and practices that you're trying to balance. Like walking a tightrope, balancing these tensions can be exhilarating and dynamic.

The Six Tensions

After evaluating the experiences and learning of several leaders, including our wives (who remain some of the best group leaders we know), we were able to identify at least six healthy tensions every small

The Six Challenges	The Six Tensions
The Learning Challenge	Truth . . . . .Life
The Development Challenge	Care . . . . .Discipleship
The Relational Challenge	Friendship . . . . . . .Accountability
The Reconciliation Challenge	Kindness . . . . .Confrontation
The Impact Challenge	Task . . . . .People
The Connection Challenge	Openness . . . . .Intimacy

group faces. The list is not exhaustive, and you may discover additional tensions along the way. But these six seem to capture much of what groups wrestle with while building community that transforms individuals and their world. So if you feel frustrated by a dilemma in your small group, perhaps we can relieve your stress. There may be no answer. It may be one of those "unsolvable problems" that place you squarely between two good things, and your job is not to find the answer but to manage the dynamic tension.

Walking the Small Group Tightrope will address these six challenges or tensions in the form of a continuum that represents the pull you feel when standing in the middle. Small group leaders reading this will gain skill in walking that tightrope. Small group members will learn to spot these tensions, adapt their perceptions and expectations of group life, and take next steps in building a community without compromise.

Every group faces these six tensions. Every group wants to create an environment in which people can learn about the faith, build truthful relationships, and grow spiritually. And every group must process disagreements and conflict, accomplish a mission, and help new people connect to the group. The six challenges are: a *learning* challenge, a *development* challenge, a *relational* challenge, a *reconciliation* challenge, an *impact* challenge, and a *connection* challenge.

Each challenge has an inherent tension. For example, the learning challenge requires a group to manage the truth-life tension. If you want people to learn truth, the truth of God's Word must connect with the story of their life. Too much story leaves no room for truth. Too much discussion of truth without connection to life can produce arrogant, puffed-up Christians who never practice what they study. We'll unpack this more later, but that gives you a sense of how we will approach the subject. Below are the six challenges and their associated tensions.

Small groups cannot thrive by focusing on either end of the continuum. They cannot choose friendship over accountability, kindness over confrontation, or task over community. Rather, effective life-giving small groups must embrace both ends of the continuum, in healthy opposition, and walk the tightrope between them toward authentic community and life change.

As we unpack these six areas your small group must manage, you'll come to a conclusion. If, in the end, you feel that small group leadership is like walking a tightrope, it means you get it.

In fact, some of the best small group leadership and participation happens on the tightrope. Each of the six areas we'll identify is a tightrope of its own, and the six taken together will keep you engaged in one of the most adventurous balancing acts of your life. As you embrace this fact and walk the tightrope, you will unleash latent energy in your group. No, it may not be easy. And it will require some work. But you are small group people, so you understand that.

Accordingly, this book contains eight chapters: this introduction, one chapter for each of the six challenges, and a conclusion. Each chapter will identify the challenge, define the inherent dynamics of the tension, describe what happens when groups lean too far toward one end of the continuum, and offer suggestions and tools so leaders can help their groups manage the polarities. After the conclusion, you'll find an appendix that includes a leader's guide for helping groups use this book with biblical material, group and personal assessments, and other exercises.

Remember, at each end of the continuum is something good, something that Scripture affirms and that groups must practice. So we'll spend time helping you understand each truth's biblical and practical implications. Then we'll explain that the tension point between the two is actually where groups find real progress and growth. Of course, the challenge for you as a leader is to help your group live there, so we'll offer helpful ideas, principles, and tools.

By the time you digest this content, you will understand how to meet these challenges by managing the tensions. The results will be life giving. Our exercises will help move your group forward in each area. And at the end of the book, we'll walk you through a summary exercise to help you formulate action steps to improve your small group's life and leadership.

By the time you complete your journey through the six healthy tensions, you will be ready to test them on your own and join the ever-adventurous, always-challenging experience of life in community. If we are right about these tensions, and this book helps you manage them more skillfully, perhaps your group will have a shot at knowing more of what Jesus prayed for when he asked the Father concerning us: "that they may be one as we are one" (John 17:11).

We have joined him in the dream that we can replicate on earth what he has known from eternity. Getting there will require walking a tightrope. So stretch those legs.

CHAPTER ONE

a change will do you good

MEETING THE LEARNING CHALLENGE BY BALANCING TRUTH AND LIFE

"The most important thing we can do in any meeting is study the Bible," said David. "I'm not sure it's the *most* important thing," responded Terry, who at age thirty-four was already a mature Christian. "After all, knowledge puffs up. It seems to me that we should put a stronger emphasis on building relationships. That's why I came to the group in the first place. We get plenty of Bible in sermons and classes."

David couldn't let that one go by without a strong, somewhat sarcastic response. "So you don't believe what Jesus taught — that the truth will set you free?" *Pretty hard to argue with Jesus*, thought David.

But Terry, a Bible college graduate, had a witty comment of her own, right out of John 5:39. "Right — he said the *truth* would set people free, not *Bible study!* Jesus rebuked arrogant Jewish leaders by saying, 'You diligently study the Scriptures because you think that by them you possess eternal life.' No one knew the Scriptures like the Pharisees — and no one's hearts were harder than theirs."

David, taking the debate up a notch, responded, "So now I'm arrogant because I believe that knowing Scripture is important! Sure, let's just toss the Bible out the window and spend all our time talking about all our problems and sharing our collective ignorance!"

Ah, yes, it's discussions like this that make small groups fun. Members arguing, personalities clashing, and conflict seeping from every corner of the room. Sort of reminds you of Jesus' group. Thomas challenging truth, Peter telling everyone what to do, Judas dipping his hand into the treasury, Simon the Zealot secretly harboring resentment against the former employee of Rome — Matthew, the tax collector — and Bartholomew sitting there, never saying a word.

Groups can get pretty animated about what they believe. The learning challenge can quickly polarize a group. Will our group focus on truth or life? Should we focus on content, the right understanding of the text, gaining the right information? Or should we spend more time helping members with personal issues, asking them to look closely at their lives, telling us their stories and being real about their needs and problems? Obviously, both truth and life are important. Here's the continuum we face when confronted with the learning challenge.

The challenge is to avoid drifting too far for too long toward one end of the continuum.

Tilting toward Truth

Fundamentally, this challenge requires understanding how Scripture study and small group curriculum help people learn the truth. How should the study guide, inductive questions, and Scripture application function in small group life?

As God's people we're committed to the truth. Both the great acclamation of Psalm 119:89, "Your word, O LORD, is eternal; it stands firm in the heavens," and God's promise through Isaiah, "so is my word that goes out from my mouth: it will not return to me empty, but will accomplish what I desire and achieve the purpose for which I sent it" (Isa. 55:11), make it clear that the truth is central to community.

An emphasis on truth apart from life will turn you into a Pharisee. A life that's not informed by truth will make you a relativist "blown here and there by every wind of teaching" (Eph. 4:14). Paul says, "For you were once darkness, but now you are light in the Lord. Live as children of light (for the fruit of the light consists in all goodness, righteousness and truth)" (Eph. 5:8–9). Look carefully at those words: "The fruit of the light consists in all goodness, righteousness *and truth.*" Truth does matter. And, according to Paul, it must connect with life.

But how do we connect truth to life in community? After all, one of your first tasks in a small group setting is to determine the role Scripture and small group study materials will play in your group.

Sadly, many little communities default to becoming a "truth group," which really means a group focused on doctrine, right and wrong answers, and the accumulation of information. The unstated group axiom is "He who knows the most, wins." Acquisition of knowledge becomes an end in itself. Members subtly buy into the lie that "information is power." Such groups reward members who are information-obsessed and secretly belittle those who are "knowledge-challenged." They view the Bible as a series of propositions and objective facts, disconnected from the life of the divine author and his audience. And so Parker Palmer writes: "The Latin root of 'objective' means 'to put against, to oppose.' In German its literal translation is 'standing-over-against-ness.' This image uncovers another quality of modern knowledge: it puts us in an adversary relationship with each other and our world. We seek knowledge in order to resist chaos, to rearrange reality, or to alter the constructions others have made. . . . Objective knowledge has fulfilled its root meaning: it has made us adversaries of ourselves."[1]

In groups a preoccupation with truth takes on a more spiritual disguise, one we often wear unwittingly. In the most extreme form, we become preoccupied with finishing the lesson. Leaders expect you to come prepared with every Bible-study blank filled in. After all, the more you know, the more raw material the Spirit has to work with when changing your heart. There is some truth in that idea. But the most dangerous form of truth is a half-truth. God wants a heart to work with, or truth has no effect. In response to the Pharisees, Jesus said, "These people honor me with their lips, but their hearts are far from me" (Matt. 15:8).

Truth groups begin at the right place when looking at Scripture or their small group curriculum. Members ask, "What does it mean?" or "What was Jesus saying when he made that statement?" The problem is that truth groups tend to stay at this level. Correct answers are rewarded by verbal affirmation from leaders ("That's a great answer!") and nonverbal cues from members as heads nod in approval.

Unfortunately, some small group study materials reinforce this mind-set by asking questions that require answers instead of prompting discussions. Groups function like classes with homework, and those who get the homework done get an A. If you didn't get the blanks filled in, you may appear lazy to the group or be embarrassed.

Truth *will* set you free, but not *all* truth, just applied truth. Jesus concluded the Sermon on the Mount with a great metaphor. In effect he says, "If you hear my words, but don't do anything with them, you are as foolish as the developer who built his Florida condominium on the sands of Miami Beach. But if you put them into practice, it's like building on a rock-solid foundation, and no storm will ever bring it down." (Okay, we are embellishing the story a bit). Truth *really* matters—but only if it moves from the head through the heart and out to the hands and feet.

Leaders: don't let your group consistently slide to the truth end of the continuum. Don't let people spend every moment of group time debating and defining truth, so that you wind up saying, "Oops, only five minutes left, so let's do a quick prayer and head on out."

If the group is unduly focused on truth and doesn't balance study by looking at life, all you will get are well-informed students. It's not a bad thing to understand and know the truth, but what about the life side?

Listing toward Life

Wooing some groups to slide to the other end of the continuum is the life emphasis. After all, it feels sooo good! People come into a small group to talk about their lives, to tell their stories, engage with one another, to learn about one another. Their lives are important, especially to them!

Life groups are rooted in experience rather than in an outside source of objective reality. This is the tell-my-story, help-me-with-my-problems, can-I-talk-about-my-issues, pray-for-me group. Good stuff, right? Gotta deal with life.

But if groups remain on this end of the continuum for too long, narcissism develops. Members begin believing a different kind of lie: "The group is all about me." The credo here is, "Small groups *of* the people, *by* the people, and *for* the people." Meeting members' needs and solving their problems is vital. But excessive absorption in each other's lives leads to an aversion to allowing truth to shape life.

Truth groups often wrestle with life without knowing what to do with it. For example, let's assume you are leading a small group of young people. They're at the age when they challenge issues and debate just about everything. They want to wrestle with life questions. A student remarks, "I'm not sure if I believe this." You wonder whether this statement reflects a genuine quest for truth or a rationalization for a rebellious attitude or lifestyle.

Pretty soon, life experience can become the arbiter of reality. Truth is replaced by what Phillip E. Johnson calls "the tyranny of prevailing opinion." This philosophy, more than ever, is captivating minds on high school and college campuses. In a *Newsweek* article, Fareed Zakaria asserted, "There has been a fundamental shift in American society, away from moral authority and toward what the sociologist Alan Wolfe calls 'moral freedom.' Wolfe finds that most Americans are actually quite concerned about morality but they want to determine for themselves how to construct a virtuous life. Less and less do they defer to the moral authority of institutions like churches."

The author then makes this statement: "Even among the religious, the dominant trend is toward individualized forms of faith in which personal autonomy plays a big role. The language of born-again Christians, for example, while deeply religious, is about personal self-discovery, not obedience to doctrine. "There is a moral majority in America,' writes Wolfe, 'It just ... wants to make up its own mind.'"[2]

This mind-set is not limited to students. Adults are infamous for putting their life experience, including what they believe about God and their sense of what he is telling them to do (not to mention their horoscope, dreams, or random opinions), on the table. Life groups look inward, implying that the goal is a well-understood self. Life groups tend to be introspective, centering on "my story, my needs, and my pain." They reward members for being real—even if they are *real wrong!* Community is built on the principle of acceptance, which means we never confront sin or hold up the mirror of truth to the face of dishonesty and deception!

Life groups take all forms. Some resemble modern-day encounter groups fitted with armchair psychologists trying to psychoanalyze one another and solve problems in a way detached from truth. Others might be called "shared ignorance" groups, in which people without knowledge try to help people without solutions. Biblical wisdom is replaced with homespun recipes for everything from how to handle marriage challenges to how to discern God's will.

There are also specialized forms of shared ignorance groups, such as the "parents-of-drooling-one-year-olds" group. Everyone wants to know how to run the child-rearing race, so they ask, "What are you doing with *your* kids?" What such groups really need is advice from someone with four children and eight grandchildren. They need truth, not just mutual sharing of woes.

Other groups drift even further from the truth end of the continuum, exhibiting a dangerous lack of biblical and theological literacy. Life overwhelms truth; falsehood creeps in. We are amazed at Christians who smiled wistfully and saw nothing wrong with Oprah

Winfrey's remarks at *Prayer for America* in New York, on September 23, 2001. As master of ceremonies, she said, "When you lose a loved one, you gain an angel whose name you know. . . . On September 11, six thousand angels were added to the spiritual roster."

Though Oprah encourages and uplifts Americans through her television broadcasts, she readily mixes truth and error, serving it up as a spiritual elixir to the masses. And people—including faithful, ignorant believers—are drinking their fill. *Christianity Today* rightly asserted, "With a congregation of 22 million viewers, Oprah Winfrey has become one of the most influential spiritual leaders in America."[3]

Still other groups masquerade as real groups but are simply coffee-klatch connections consisting of social conversation. It may resemble a chat by the watercooler at work or sound like a group of underchallenged guys in the fitness-center locker room. Not a lot of transformation happening. But you will find plenty of opinions and ideas. A Christian version of this can soon become a "prayer and share" group. But everyone knows that's code for a "prayer and gossip" group. People tell each other stories and the latest news, pray to let God in on the drama, and head out the door looking for someone to spill the beans to.

Before you recognize what is happening, group members become so interested in connecting with each other's lives that the truth plays an increasingly nominal role in the process. Trying to interrupt the flow of life-on-life connection can feel like a violation.

When is it okay for a group to have a more social focus? Groups of all varieties face this question, whether they meet in the evening or early morning. I (Bill) know, because right now I lead a men's group that meets at 6:30 A.M. at the church. Sometimes guys show up looking like they need a caffeine transfusion. It takes a few moments before we can get into deep truth, so the temptation is to "go social" and sip another cup of coffee, keeping discussion at the surface level for an hour or so, then head out for the day. This isn't wrong, but it can be dangerous to drift there week after week. The desire for relational connection can overwhelm the need for discussing transforming truth.

When some pastors think of life groups they envision people doctrinally adrift, reading the latest Danielle Steele novel, watching Shirley MacLaine videos, and singing "the answer, my friend, is blowin' in the wind" between servings of granola and tofu. Well, maybe it's not that bad. But the concern is valid. Groups might have meaningful prayer, activities, and community but lack a scriptural center that functions as a compass to inform decisions and ward off error.

Can a group have meaningful, God-honoring experiences without doing Bible study? Yes, indeed. We have groups that serve in a variety of capacities to extend hope and help to the poor and needy. Some of those groups have no official Bible study component. They are effective, but they would be more robust if a truth-based discussion were included in the process. Leaders of such groups must guide members to classes, personal Bible study, and regular pulpit teaching to ensure that their lives are exposed to biblical truth. The temptation is to use activity and social interaction as an excuse to avoid the truth, because the truth calls us to change.

In the same way, some groups are initially organized for the purpose of studying and understanding Scripture. Members are eager to learn new doctrines and probe the depths of God's profound and soul-piercing Word. That is a great thing. We have groups at Willow (and have seen them in other churches where we have served) that focus on Bible study methods. Learning to study Scripture is a wonderful and useful skill for any believer and will bear much fruit in life. But the danger lies in the possibility that studying and dissecting truth will become an end in itself. Members may be informed but never really *transformed.* The missing life component, which exhorts people to become doers and not just hearers of the word, is conspicuously absent.

Spiritual Transformation: Where Truth Meets Life

So on the one end we have truth, the transcendent reality of God's Word. And on the other end we have life, with all its real problems, needs, and issues. What if we could bring these two things together to walk the tightrope between them?

We would land in the area we call "spiritual transformation." Because that's the place where truth really meets life. It looks like this:

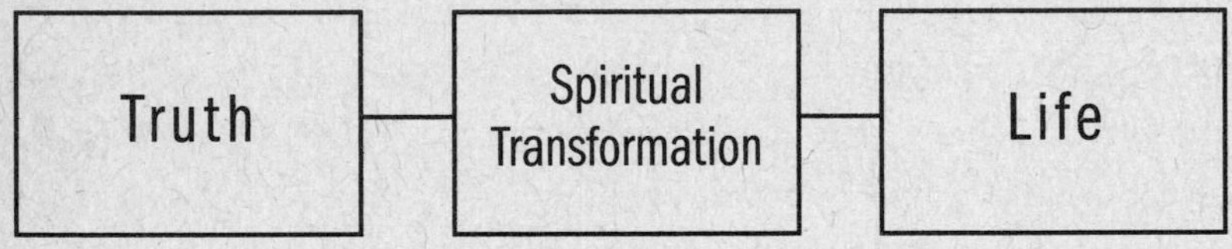

Both truth and life are needed. Spiritual transformation occurs when truth meets life and must be the outcome of any group. This is why we call it the *learning* challenge. It is about truth that engages life and produces spiritual growth in the community of Christ followers. Therefore the truth must become personal and relational. Parker Palmer states it powerfully: "In him [Christ], truth, once understood as abstract, principled, propositional, suddenly takes on a human face and human frame. In Jesus, the disembodied 'word' takes flesh and walks among us. Jesus calls us to truth, but not in the forms of creeds and theologies or worldviews. His call to truth is a call to community — with him, with each other, with creation and its Creator. If what we know is abstract, impersonal, apart from us, it cannot be truth, for truth involves a vulnerable, faithful, and risk-filled interpenetration of the knower and the known."[4]

For you, as a small group leader, the learning challenge is about walking a tightrope—to stand between the tension of truth and life and do both. That is, make sure truth is very present in your meetings, but also make sure that truth is brought to bear on life in community. You must call members to open their lives to one another so they can be changed.

We talk a lot about that at Willow Creek. We want to see people's lives changed, and for that to happen, truth has to meet life. That's how people become "fully devoted followers of Christ."

You can see the tension in the situations we have described. You live with it every day in your group. We want to help you walk the truth-life tightrope in your group, so that truth will meet life and you will land in the life-giving connection called spiritual transformation. That's where we want to be, isn't it?

There's great potential for spiritual transformation when God's truth connects with small group members' lives. Small group leaders can create an interactive, dynamic environment for truth-life encounters by:

- Connecting Scripture with story
- Turning questions into discussions
- Practicing active listening
- Varying learning styles

Scripture and Story

When I (Bill) had been at Willow Creek for about a year, my family headed back to Texas for Christmas to spend a few days in Dallas with friends and a few days in San Antonio with my wife's family. We arrived in Dallas, but our luggage was lost, most likely on a plane to El Paso. This wasn't such a bad deal except our three-year-old son desperately needed a change of clothes, and his bag was lost. So after arranging things with the airline, we headed to the home of friends who'd left town.

They'd given us their home's security code, but one of us lost it — I can't say who. Finally, we remedied the problem and stopped at a restaurant. My wife had been struggling with a throat virus in Chicago, and during dinner she lost her voice. The next day I lost my wallet.

But the real deal breaker occurred in San Antonio after celebrating the holidays with family. All our bags were packed; it was early morn. Our ride was waiting, blowing his horn. Oh babe, we hate to go. We're leavin' on a jet plane; don't know when we'll be back again. (Oops, got carried away there.) Anyway, we were ready to head to the airport, only to discover we had lost our tickets. I know what you are thinking: *Never travel with the Donahues!*

Ever lost anything of value? How does it feel? What emotions fill your soul when you can't find your paycheck, or your keys are missing, or your two-year-old has drifted from view in a crowded mall? Terror? Fear? Sheer panic? My guess is that you identify with my story — because my story is similar to yours. You know loss and grief and panic and guilt and pain.

Jesus used stories because he knew people. He understood their hearts and connected truth with life by using stories (parables) to drive home his point. Sometimes the meaning was clear, sometimes it was a bit hidden so that only the openhearted learner could absorb the truth tucked away in the story.

Groups grow when Scripture and story collide with members' lives, demanding that they shape their ongoing story in conformity with God's story, becoming more like Christ in the process. Thus truth and life are integrated in the group's learning process.

In case you're wondering (and you probably are, because you identify with stories), we found the security code to the home, received all our luggage, and Gail recovered her voice while still in Dallas. My wallet was wet but lying right where it had fallen next to the curb where I had parked. But we never did find those plane tickets. Thankfully, the airline made it all work out so we could return home, vowing never to take a family vacation for the rest of our lives.

It's great to find something of value that you have lost. That's why Jesus, in describing how much lost people matter to God, told stories instead of simply making his point in a proposition. He didn't say, "Lost people are important to me and should be important to you as well! Write that down in your notebooks." Rather, Jesus talked about a lost coin, a lost sheep, and a lost son, always bringing the story to a climax that yields a shocking picture of God. Jesus describes how a Jewish father broke with all custom and protocol to wildly pursue the prodigal son who offended and disgraced him before the entire village. The power of story brings truth to life, not only convicting listeners' minds but also captivating their emotions.

Groups can leverage the power of story as they study Scripture. First, of course, the Bible has many stories and parables for discussion. But even when studying material like Ephesians 1, where waves of truth pound the shores of your mind in every verse, stories can be integrated into the context. Group members' personal stories can illustrate the study topic, or at least open hearts and minds to learning about the topic. Leaders can also use news articles or "human interest" stories, as well as video clips or stories on tape.

Many of you may have chuckled as you read my disastrous story above, but you also can relate to Jesus' story because of it. You know what it's like to lose something precious and to celebrate finding it. So even if you cannot enter fully into the first-century story, my current version acts as a bridge, helping you connect truth with life.

Turn Questions into Discussions

What is the purpose of asking a question? Getting an answer, right? Yes — except in small groups. The purpose of a question in a small group is to create a discussion. What happens when you ask a question that demands a specific answer and someone gives the answer? There is no discussion. These are called closed-ended questions, questions designed to elicit data. They rarely create a dynamic interaction, because once you get the facts — end of discussion!

Jesus wanted to befuddle the Pharisees, so he asked them a multiple-choice question about John the Baptist: "John's baptism — where did it come from? Was it from heaven, or from men?" (Matt. 21:25). Which was it? They had only two options; that's a fifty-fifty chance. But the Pharisees were stumped, because they thought, *If we say it's from men, boy, we're in trouble because the people believe John is a prophet. If we say it's from God, they'll say, "Then why don't you believe him?"* So they stuck their heads in the sand and made no reply. End of discussion. Similarly, in small groups, fear of being wrong kills a discussion every time.

Closed-ended questions are good and have a purpose. But that purpose is to elicit answers, not create discussions. Our goal in a small group is to try to engage people in discussions. How do you do that?

Here are a few tips. First, *begin with open-ended questions that invite insights, opinions, and personal reflection*. For instance, "What would it look like to really love our neighbor the way Jesus has taught?" "What thoughts and feelings might the woman at the well have experienced as she interacted with Jesus?" These questions have no correct answers but begin to help members probe into their own lives as they relate to the passage being discussed.

Next, *make sure that your questions become focused and personal*. For example, let's say that your group is doing a study on 1 Corinthians 10:13: "No temptation has seized you except what is common to man. And God is faithful; he will not let you be tempted beyond what you can bear. But when you are tempted, he will also provide a way out so that you can stand up under it."

The truth-focused group tends to respond by asking, "What does God promise us when we are tempted?" And the right answer is, of course, "a way of escape." Maybe the curriculum or leader will follow with, "And what are some ways that we can escape temptation?" Answers might include running from it, quoting Scripture like Jesus did when Satan confronted him, and being accountable to a close friend. All these things are true and helpful.

Members nod their heads, and a few may jot ideas in their journals or Bibles. The problem is that in these questions truth has only begun to meet life. The discussion could be taken further, depending on the spiritual and emotional barometer of the group.

To turn a question into a discussion, the leader must ask an additional and different kind of question, such as, "When have you felt most trapped, like there's no way of escape from a temptation?" Such questions require discussion, or at least open up the possibility of discussion, because now people have to engage.

The question above is a good question, because it's reasonably safe; it doesn't ask people to bare their souls about sin. Yet it invites discussion about when members have felt trapped by temptation, as if there were no escape. Another good question might be, "At what point emotionally do you become most vulnerable to temptation; which step on the slippery slope starts you down the path of no return?" Breaking into groups of two or three may stimulate conversation, because smaller groups make people feel safer and offer them more chances to think and feel deeply.

When your group grapples with these kinds of questions, someone may choose to disclose something they have held back until now. Open-ended questions invite this kind of response, because they give members permission to go deeper. Then the adventure into spiritual transformation begins, especially because members' thoughts will be bounded by the truth from which the discussion has emerged.

Many small group curricula include the question, "What do you think Jesus meant when he said . . . ?" This basic question is good, but not personal. I can talk all day about what I think Jesus meant when he spoke. So what? It is conjecture. It also opens the door for shared ignorance to dominate.

It's best to state the obvious truth or necessary facts before asking your question. For example, "Scholars agree that Jesus was referring here to the Pharisees' hard hearts. What must we do to help each other battle hard-heartedness in our relationships?"

For truth to meet life, the small group has to move from general content to more personal questions. Some curriculum questions need only minor adjustments or a follow-up question to move the group. Putting in this extra work is worth it.

The third way to turn questions into discussions is to *make your discussion more interactive and creative*. We know some of you small group leaders are saying, "Oh, there's the creative word. They're going to ask me to do stuff I'm not good at. I'm not that creative." Well, you know what? Designing interactive discussions sounds challenging, but we have easy tips for getting more interactive and innovative.

Our years of working with adults have reminded us that adults are really just grown-up kids who still relate to elementary-school experiences. For example, when discussing scriptural metaphors of the church as a building or a plant, you can hand out construction paper and markers. Have group members team up to create their image of the metaphor. This isn't about artwork; it's about process. Group participation gives people time to reflect on what God says about the church.

While studying about "putting on the full armor of God," Lynn and I (Russ) had everyone make a full "armor" outfit from old newspapers. Not only was it more fun than a dull discussion about parsing hard-to-comprehend ideas; it also proved to be a great memory aid! For the first time, even veteran Christians reckoned with the implications of how they could practice this truth in their lives.

Creativity and interaction generate fun, reduce tension, open hearts, and engage people. It doesn't take much to turn a topic into a game or debate. You might even create your own version of popular game shows like Jeopardy, Family Feud, or Wheel of Fortune. You'll find that trying to process, organize, and present truth for others helps people learn and remember biblical truths — especially when groups review studies from past meetings. Remember to involve everyone and delegate some leadership to your apprentice.

If your group has six or more people and you want it to be more interactive, you'll have to divide into subgroups. We don't know how to get people to engage without sometimes getting them into groups of two or three. When you have eight or more people in your groups, you'll still want to have everyone share together, but size will prohibit in-depth sharing. Consider forming subgroups on occasion unless your group has four members or less attending a given meeting.

Vary Learning Styles

Some people are readers, some listeners, some doers, and some are watchers. Everyone learns differently, and different truths require different kinds of presentation or interaction. By varying learning formats in a group, you encourage creativity and help more people connect truth with life.

But often we get into a rut in our small groups. It's really easy to fall into the let's-read-and-discuss, let's-read-and-discuss, let's-read-and-discuss rhythm, week after week, month after month. Sometimes it's better to greet members with "Hey, keep your coats on. We need to go out somewhere." Simply changing the routine, or varying the style or venue, can improve the learning.

We've seen powerful examples of the effect of being sensitive to members' different learning styles. Visual learners need to see pictures. I (Russ) will always remember when our leader brought in Henri Nouwen's book *The Return of the Prodigal Son,* which discusses the Luke 15 story by examining Rembrandt's painting *The Return of the Prodigal Son*. As someone read excerpts, we could all look at the classic images of the father embracing his son, with the older brother looking on.

Perhaps some people need refreshed vision. They need someone to cast a new vision—give them a picture—of what God says their life could look like. That picture produces a hunger in them for their lives to be changed by truth.

My (Russ) wife, Lynn, is great at using music to help auditory learners. She recently facilitated a meeting meant to connect women into various prayer dimensions. Her talk drew on vast biblical content about prayer. But she wanted to engage these women with God. So she allowed the group to listen to different styles of recorded music. Auditory learners could contemplate God's greatness through majestic music, reflect on sin via soulful tunes, feel thankful with celebrative lyrics, and intercede while listening to a song about caring for others. It was great for them to hear something more than spoken words.

Kinesthetic learners need to touch what you're talking about. You can creatively reach them through crafts, projects, and other hands-on activities.

Don't overlook the potential of role-playing. During the Christmas season, one family group at Willow spent three weeks acting out stories—one week as Zechariah, Elizabeth, Mary, and Joseph; the next week as Mary, Joseph, and the shepherds; and the last week as Jesus' family and the wise men. This exercise drew on many learning styles.

Others, like me (Bill), are experiential learners. We need to do something to learn. When I wanted my group to value understanding and serving the poor, I didn't just teach about it. Instead, we piled into a minivan and visited a homeless shelter. Seeing poverty firsthand inspired people to think about how to serve these folks. "There are twenty-three beds, and I count only seventeen blankets," one member remarked. "Yeah, that's a problem," I responded calmly. "Maybe we ought to get them some blankets?" he remarked. "Yeah, good idea," I said, trying to hide my enthusiasm for what was happening.

Another guy asked, "What's with the ceiling here? Actually, there isn't one. It's just shredded fibers. Somebody needs to put a ceiling in here." My response: "You're right, somebody needs to do that." "Well, maybe we could help," he volunteered. "You know, that's an idea we need to discuss as a group," I offered. More learning took place in ten minutes than in two weeks of study on the subject. This lesson required experiential learning.

Practice Active Listening

Leaders are often better talkers than listeners. We guide, direct, teach, motivate, challenge, and exhort. Less often, we listen. When we *really* listen—with our ears and with our eyes—we can seize holy moments by recognizing that God is at work and the Holy Spirit has just grabbed the agenda. The following situations may signal a change of heart, conviction of sin, or a comfort-zone disruption.

- *A change in the mood of the group.* Does the mood suddenly turn from happy to quiet and reflective? This may be a cue that a holy moment is near. Perhaps a statement has rocked the group, or a member has just opened up about pain or frustration.
- *Body language and facial expressions.* Are people leaning in and engaging or slouching back? Are they thinking about yesterday's confrontation with the boss or solving a problem they have to face when they get home? Do their expressions communicate confusion, sadness, guilt, or lack of interest? Or are they wide-eyed while hearing about God's wrath for the first time? Faces can tell you a lot. Remember that distraction sometimes means

the discussion has struck a chord, taking people deeper into hearts, souls, and minds.

- *Tone of voice.* What are people saying by *how* they speak? What does their volume and intensity level say? Voices betray what's really going on. Here's an easy test. Say the following sentences, emphasizing the word in italics each time. I *love* you. I love *you*. *I* love you? *Yeah*, I luv ya. Now, most men won't hear a difference, but women generally pick it up pretty well. And they have great memories for this sort of thing! Tone of voice makes a huge difference.
- *Change in habits or behaviors.* How people behave in new settings may show whether God is at work. Say someone shares how she has begun to meet with God at her workplace, during a few minutes at lunch. Instead of simply saying, "That's great!" a leader who is truly listening will say, "Tell us more about that. What are you discovering, and what prompted this change? We can all be encouraged by what you are doing." Engage the group and make note of these changes.

Besides listening to more than your members' words, you'll want to be attentive to what God might be doing among you. Has he just put his finger on a truth to be reckoned with, a person to pray for, a conflict to process, or confusion to clarify? Certainly, we can't know the mind of God or detect his every action, but we can be attentive and risk exploring observations and feelings, checking with the group to see what requires our focus in the moment.

Modeling active listening for the group will make it easier for them to do the same, seizing those moments when God is at work in a heart or in a community of believers.

As you carefully walk the truth-life tightrope, you will see the fruit of your efforts—spiritual transformation in members' lives. You will develop what we could call "a spiritual transformation–focused group," in which members diligently seek to know the truth, not just about themselves, but about God as well. The focus is on how the truth about God connects with the truth about each life in the circle, as members strive together to promote growth and change. Bringing truth and life together requires groups to maintain a dynamic tension.

I (Russ) have watched as others, especially Bill, have developed most of Willow Creek's curricula. They've worked really hard to create more engaging questions that will generate discussion. They've used many learning styles to help leaders creatively meet the learning challenge.

What if you're weak on the truth end of the continuum? Try selecting a new curriculum that has a life-changing focus, one that would engage people in wrestling with biblical truth. We've intimately field-tested the truth-life combination of dozens of study guides.

The Interactions series, for example, relates major topics of faith to real life. The New Community series does the same with books of the Bible, as do the Bible 101 series and the Spiritual Transformation series with biblical truth and spiritual formation. The Tough Questions series and the Reality Check series engage spiritual seekers in managing the truth-life dynamic.

If your group is strong on the truth end but weak on the life end of the continuum, you'll want to increase their awareness of the Holy Spirit. It's about observing what God is doing. Your small group isn't building this community alone. The Holy Spirit really is active in your midst, and he will speak to each of you.

Don't allow opening prayer to become perfunctory or passé. Hold hands, get on your knees, or try other simple changes to recognize the potential for the movement of the Holy Spirit during this time of prayer. You might even start your meeting by praying for each other rather than waiting till the final five minutes. Then during your biblical discussion, application might get more attention, since everyone is more aware of life situations and Spirit promptings.

Choosing a curriculum that exposes people's lives to the Bible is especially challenging for task groups — and in chapter 6 we'll specifically address the dynamics unique to task groups. For now, we'll acknowledge that task groups must find creative ways to promote interactive, life-changing discussion during their limited meeting times.

As you meet the learning challenge and move discussions to the place where truth meets life, you will be prepared for the next balancing act — the developmental challenge. We will walk that tightrope together in the next chapter.

CHAPTER TWO

are we treating wounds or training soldiers?

MEETING THE DEVELOPMENT CHALLENGE BY BALANCING CARE AND DISCIPLESHIP

I (Russ) was raised in the home of a Navigator — the Navy SEALs of the spiritual world. These folks present a determined "this is discipleship at its best" image and tend toward the macho end of parachurch discipleship organizations. That's not a derogatory analogy; these people know we are in a high-stakes battle for people's souls and take discipleship seriously.

Navigators' founder, Dawson Trotman, was well known for his personal discipline and rigor. He emphasized Bible study, Scripture memorization, and life-on-life ministry — first leading students and military personnel to Christ and then guiding them to mature in faith.

So when my dad came to Christ through the Navigators while in the navy, he was hooked on their ministry model. We had all the Bible study guides, memory systems, and other tools necessary for building up men and women. As a young man, I had a front row seat to seeing the profound impact my dad made through personal and small group discipleship activities.

Defining the Discipleship Challenge

My dad's example didn't mean I had an easy time deciding to follow Christ. It wasn't until age fourteen that I made a personal decision to end some adolescent rebellion and give God control of my life.

About a year after I became a Christian, I was sitting in the library at my public high school when a couple guys approached and asked if they could show me something. Seeking to avoid homework at all costs, I agreed. They asked me to read a brief article, and a conversation ensued. One guy, a friend of mine, asked, "Russ, are you a Christian?" "Yes, I am," I finally admitted. They hooked me up with an on-campus representative of Campus Crusade for Christ (Campus Crusade, for short), and so began my second dose of discipleship intensity.

Intense Discipleship

Campus Crusade is fiercely evangelistic and very committed to initial discipleship using personal and small group approaches. Soon I was meeting regularly with these guys for Bible study and spiritual discussions.

Later, as a high school junior, I got involved with a small group led one summer by college-aged alumni from our high school. It was a solid group, but the leaders feared their hard work would come to nothing when summer ended. They asked me to carry the ball. One leader promised to mentor me. This was no ordinary mentoring relationship. My mentor came out of InterVarsity Christian Fellowship (IVCF), another committed discipleship organization. Throw in my time attending Bible college, and you can bet I was fully schooled on small group approaches to discipleship.

But one small group experience threw me a curve. In 1987, Lynn and I started a small group to disciple three young couples in our church. We were living in North Dakota, one of those places you are remembered for being from. (When we arrived at Willow Creek, Lee Strobel asked me if I had turned out the lights when I left!) Like the other couples, we were transplants with no family in the area, so we naturally gravitated toward each other.

Lynn and I were intent on getting the discipleship job done with these young Christians. But in contrast to the intense discipleship we desired to provide, this group spent loads of energy caring for one another. We supported one another through difficult life challenges, functioning like the extended families we had left behind.

We're supposed to disciple these people, I thought. *What am I supposed to do about all the time spent caring for one another?* And soon people were expecting *me* to care for *them*. I only knew how to push the discipleship button, at least as I understood discipleship. But the more I pushed, the more they wanted a caring, nurturing environment void of the intensity associated with many discipleship models. As I fumbled around, Lynn put her spiritual gifts of shepherding and encouragement in play, and we learned how to invite the group to the community party.

These people challenged my narrow perception of small group life, my belief that it was just about discipleship (traditionally defined by some as a series of skills and disciplines to be mastered). For the first time in my leadership journey, I was challenged to look at both ends of the development continuum. We know that disciples are supposed to be caring (John 13:34–35), and we all know that mutual care leads to spiritual growth. The tension arises in the mind of the small group leader, who as the shepherd of the group, must constantly balance the nurturing, caring requirements with the responsibility to challenge people in other areas of growth (like Scripture memory, spiritual disciplines, and evangelistic activity). So here's the continuum.

Given how I earned my small group leader stripes, I was ignorant of the emphasis that needed to be placed on the care component.

Caring Enough to Care

Though I share some of what Russ experienced, I (Bill) remember my first foray into a group that had drifted too far toward the care/nurture side, especially during meetings. The leader asked the fourteen of us — couples and singles, some older, some with newborns, some hoping for marriage — if we had any needs. One woman spoke up, sharing her current relational pain with male friends. She was certain she was driving men away but didn't know why. For the next half hour, members offered understanding, compassion, counsel, and prayer. I thought, *Wow, this group really ministered to her. I am glad I'm here — especially if I ever hit the wall like that!*

Those warm thoughts quickly cooled when the leader said, "Alright, let's continue around the circle and see how we can meet the needs of each person here tonight." I quickly did the math. *Let's see, fourteen people times thirty minutes per person is . . . seven hours! This isn't a meeting; it's a small group marathon!* At the three-hour mark, roughly 10 P.M., the leader said, "That was an incredible time of ministry and sharing. Now let's move on to our Bible study time together." *Bible study! Now? Next they'll want my firstborn child!* I began searching for my car keys or a cyanide capsule but found neither. It was a long night.

I really loved these people — and still do, keeping up friendships that span years and miles — and I respected and admired the leader, but the group had drifted and was spending too much time on care, especially for the group's size. Meetings that began at 6 or 7 P.M. were ending well after midnight. The leader, feeling the responsibilities laid out above, was trying to do everything during the small group meeting (especially since we met only once every three weeks). People were becoming increasingly focused on healing and prayer (good things), causing us to extend the meeting time so we could also address learning and growth issues. Ironically, I began to care less about engaging with the group outside of meetings because we had done so much during the meeting! Too much emphasis on intensive pastoral care for each person was decreasing our ability to pursue other discipleship priorities.

So What Is the Answer?

Should leaders focus on care or discipleship? Correct — the answer is a resounding "Both!" It's like walking a tightrope, balancing two very good things and holding them in tension.

Perhaps previous small group experiences have shaped your understanding of the leader's role in a small group. Should a leader emphasize a loving, caring environment in which people can bring pain and find healing, or is it a leader's purpose to produce committed followers of Christ? The answer again: "Both!"

The truth-life continuum addresses the role of curriculum or Bible study in a group. The development challenge stretches the tightrope between care and discipleship, two things every leader must model and attend to in a small group. Attention, group members! Ever wonder exactly what your leader is supposed to do besides start and end on time and get the chips and cookies ready? Now you know.

When a leader creates an environment that is both caring and developmental, he or she is practicing what we at Willow Creek have come to call "intentional shepherding."

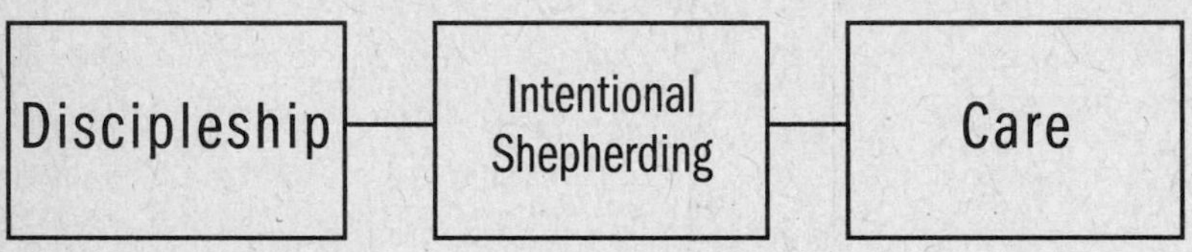

We admit the term "intentional shepherding" is somewhat redundant, since the Bible is clear that good shepherds are intentional. But we use the two-word phrase because most people think of shepherding as *reactive* ministry, in which leaders respond to the needs of the sheep as they arise. In contrast, intentional shepherding is very *proactive*. And it combines the discipleship and care components of your group experience.

Groups that focus on only the disciplines of discipleship tend to attract the strong and prepare soldiers for battle. Groups that spend an inordinate amount of energy on caregiving tend to focus on the needs of the weak and hurting, providing a strong sense of family for them. Both are good; we need armies *and* families. Both are essential in kingdom work. The challenge for a leader is how to guide a group to accomplish both in the context of small group life.

Overcoming Leader Bias

Every small group leader has a bias on the development continuum. Experience, personality, or gift mix may make a leader feel most comfortable operating at one end of the continuum. Leaders must recognize their bias, or they run the risk of falling off the tightrope.

Once you discern your bias, you can identify steps to fight the drift. We've developed a diagram to help leaders identify their own developmental bias in leading small groups.

Discipleship		
	Teach	Shepherd
	Connect	Nurture
	Caring	

Here's how it works. As you focus more on discipleship, you travel upward on the diagram. As you increase the caring activity of group life, you move to the right. We all begin at the lower left corner, simply connecting people to our little community. But then a leader begins to lean toward his or her bias. An incomplete view of discipleship tends to create a teaching and instructional environment, landing in the upper left quadrant. The care champions will tend to drift toward the lower right, creating a nurturing feel.

Neither experience is wrong or bad. We are simply acknowledging reality. Leaders have biases, so the issue is whether you recognize your bias and compensate as you lead.

As a group matures beyond simply connecting people, you might find you're heavier on discipleship and that the care component, the nurturing side, hasn't taken place yet. Your group's personality will tend to be in the upper left quadrant, in the teaching category.

If you're strong on nurturing, and there's a lot of love and support in the group but you really haven't set the intentional discipling component in place yet, you'll land in the nurturing category. Once you recognize that tendency, you can determine whether change is needed. If you can strive, over time, to invest in both areas, you'll land in the shepherding quadrant.

Take a look at the small group you lead right now, and make your best judgment about the fundamental nature of your leadership. Which quadrant best describes your strength? Then, thinking as a small group leader, ponder which quadrant best describes your group.

Russ and I (Bill) tend to drift toward the discipleship end of the continuum, at least in the classic sense in which it has been understood. We were taught that disciples are *learners,* which is technically true. But our Western thinking quickly translated this into primarily intellectual learning and information gathering, versus learning in relationships, in service, and in love. I strive to move my Thursday morning men's small group into the shepherding box, but because I have teaching gifts, I'm likely to give the group that teacher-student feel, turning the group into a classroom. It's not that we don't have a caring community, but that's where I know I have to grow and develop. So my current men's group would have the *X* right here, pushing toward the shepherding quadrant but still in the teaching box:

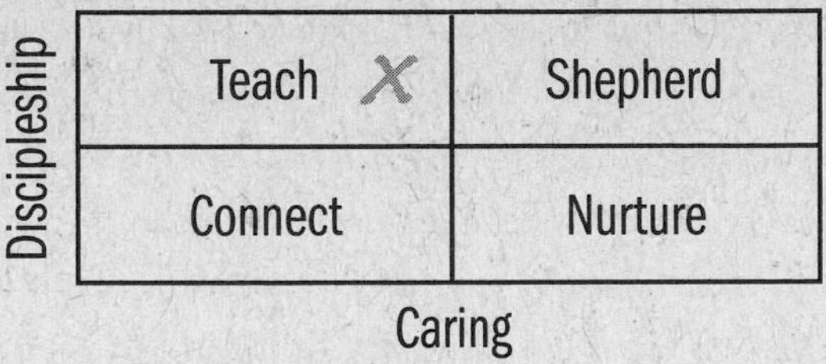

Discipleship

Teach X	Shepherd
Connect	Nurture

Caring

If you tend more toward the care end of the continuum, your *X* will be in the lower right corner, because your group will have a more nurturing feel. Diagnosing your current situation prompts you to consider change. Awareness is 70 percent of the deal here, and when you notice your bias taking over, you can adjust. Remember, in a given meeting you can land on one end of the continuum or the other. We are talking about the ongoing feel and emphasis of a group, not of an individual meeting.

It's possible that even after meeting for a few months, a group can be low on discipleship *and* on care. People are simply connecting, playing in the shallow end of the pool. Use this diagram as a diagnostic tool and be honest about what's driving low discipleship and low care. Low discipleship results from the absence of a good curriculum or direction. A group should ask, "What kind of person are we trying to produce? What should we be doing together to help us grow?" A group that remains low on care may simply not be getting to know each other. The next chapter will provide some help in this area. To move beyond the quadrant of connecting, choose a curriculum, set some growth goals, and identify areas of personal need using relationship-building exercises (a number of these are listed in *Leading Life-Changing Small Groups*). Then you will be able to make some progress toward meeting the development challenge.

We have observed that some leaders fear moving into the shepherding arena because they will have to be responsible, accountable, and emotionally engaged. That takes effort and may be messy. We hate to admit it, but sometimes we think, *If we really start shepherding, we really have to* be *there.* It's safer not to be there for some of us, isn't it? While we don't go so far as thinking we don't want to get too close to people, we nevertheless may subtly fear intimacy or emotional vulnerability.

A couple in our church is facing this issue. She wants intimacy, and he is fearful. He knows it means more availability on his part and facing some of his pain. Rather than do that, however, he withdraws. So we are trying to coach him to set levels of vulnerability. Take one step at a time. Test the waters. And give feedback to his wife as to how fast he can move into deeper relationship with her. It is scary for him, but he is making progress. It is often scary for group leaders as well, but we must continue to move forward. God calls us to overcome and work through this fear, which is common even among the best of leaders. After all, God had to tell Joshua five times to "be strong and courageous."

Despite making progress on this issue, we have to admit that sometimes we're afraid to go too far into caring, because it involves a commitment to a person and ultimately to a group. And we have busy lives and wonder whether we can really provide genuine care for someone. History says we can, but sometimes we remain reluctant to put our hearts out there again, fearful that they might get damaged or that a needy person might emotionally drain us.

One leader we know has the opposite problem. She is terrific at caring for people but rarely challenges people to their next level of spiritual maturity. In part, her own insecurities make her more comfortable remaining in the caregiving mode that keeps her one up on her group. She knows that being intentional about group growth means work—more study and preparation. She must face this reality, honestly look at where she puts the *X* on the diagram, and ponder why. What will it take to move beyond her insecurities to a more balanced approach to shepherding?

One of our groups got a wake-up call when a member challenged some of the complacency that had set in. "Here's the bottom line for me," he said. "It seems we've been going around in circles. We care about each other, and that's part of it—a big part. But we have to ask ourselves, 'Are we moving forward, pressing on toward Christlikeness in other areas as well?' That is why I participate. If our group does not help us pursue growth together, we are wasting our time." Needless to say, this generated a lively discussion. A few other members felt the same. People were losing interest because the leader was not pushing the group to the edge of spiritual growth. As a result, the leader got more intentional about the group goals and the materials being chosen for study and discussion.

That is what we want: to get care and discipleship working together, to walk the tightrope toward intentional shepherding.

Assessing Group Bias

Though we've focused on the leader's role so far, group bias plays a substantive role in the development challenge. Members have expectations for leaders. Spiritual maturity and emotional needs shape what groups expect from leaders, as have former small group leaders, parents, pastors, teachers, and other authority figures.

New Christians may view the leader as a spiritual guide and mentor. They look for direction, teaching, and answers to basic questions.

But the leader may tend toward providing nurture and care, frustrating the member who wants more structure for learning and challenges to grow. Other members may look to the leader for increasing levels of care or for the group to foster an environment of nurture. Either way, the tightrope will wobble. When group members prefer one end but the leader has a bias toward the continuum's other end, disappointment may set in.

The group's conflicting needs, desires, and unexpressed wishes further complicate the mix. As the leader responds to the care needs of one member, those seeking spiritual maturity may feel slighted. Unless these issues are discussed openly and group expectations are clarified, tension will build and frustration will reign. And the leader will wonder, *What's up with these people?*

The following exercise can help your group assess expectations for the shepherding environment—including the leader's actions and the group's responsibilities. You'll find out how each member views your small group community and where they see the group on the care-discipleship diagram.

First, hand out copies of the diagram above (or draw it on a large sheet of paper) and explain what it means. Ask each member to make two *X* marks. The first should reflect current group reality; the second should reflect personal expectations. Then ask each person to share what they have marked and why. This exercise may trip chaotic discussion. However, it will reveal reasons for unstated tensions and give everyone a chance to state their expectations.

Finally, move the discussion into the intentional shepherding quadrant. Compare thoughts on how both discipleship and care in the group can move in the direction needed to meet the needs and desires of the group, while accounting for each person's bias.

The day you bring discipleship and care together, and that's what we're all striving for, you'll be firmly planted on the tightrope. Once you see the new challenge—to hold expanded discipleship and increased care in dynamic tension—you'll have a shot at landing in the intentional shepherding box. Granted, it's much easier to talk about intentional shepherding than to do it.

At Home in the Midpoint: Intentional Shepherding

There are many tools and training courses that might be useful in helping your small group meet the development challenge. You'll find many versions of shepherding plans meant to help leaders balance the care-discipleship tension. In *Leading Life-Changing Small Groups,* we have used a basic plan built around our five Gs of spiritual development. These five words or phrases function as a developmental framework to help people measure their spiritual progress and assess opportunities for growth.

Grace. We want people to experience saving grace, understand its full measure, and then extend it to others. Grace means coming to grips with our sin before a holy God and receiving Christ's substitutionary work on our behalf. When groups truly understand how amazing God's grace is, their hearts fill with love for those who've not yet experienced it.

Growth. To achieve maturity, groups must commit themselves to those practices, relationships, and experiences that will bring them into the presence of Christ and transform them into his image. Practicing spiritual disciplines, both individually and as a group, will propel your group toward greater spiritual growth and power.

Groups. We refer here to the value of community in both small groups and the larger group, as experienced through corporate worship. People need to participate at both group levels to truly connect with Christ and one another. It is exciting to see many small group members sitting together in church and taking classes and serving together. They are as committed to the larger community as they are to their small group.

Gifts. As Christ followers, we respond to the Holy Spirit's work in our lives and, as we grow, start to give something back to the body. Paul discusses this kind of servanthood in 1 Corinthians 12. God rejoices when his followers use their spiritual gifts to serve the kingdom and minister to those outside the church.

Good Stewardship. Eventually we grow enough to share not just what we *have* but all of who we *are*—our time, talents, treasure, and even our lives. As Paul says in 1 Thessalonians 2:8, "We loved you so much that we were delighted to share with you not only the gospel of God but our lives as well, because you had become so dear to us." Groups that practice good stewardship remember Christ's blessings in their own lives and eagerly share their blessings with others. They share themselves not only in their own church but anywhere they can meet a need—locally, nationally, and internationally.

Leaders who need to increase the care component of shepherding can tap into Intentional Shepherding Training.[1] This training course uses a four-step process to bring greater care into the developmental challenge, while ensuring increased discipleship.

Overall, any intentional shepherding process will involve four steps: building relationships, assessing needs, developing a plan, and monitoring progress.

Build Authentic Relationships

Initially, you won't be able to build an authentic relationship with each person in your group, so the leader and apprentice leader should develop their relationship first, modeling authenticity and the pursuit of spiritual growth. These two leaders can then begin to build similar relationships with the group members. Ultimately, members can engage with one another, not needing to rely on the leaders alone. For intentional shepherding to work, members need someone to take a personal interest in them and their lives.

Paul did this with Priscilla and Aquila, whom he met in Corinth while making tents with them (Acts 18:1–4). Later, as they grew in faith, he modeled ministry before them and took them with him to Syria and Ephesus (18:18–20). Then he left them in Ephesus as house church leaders. There they mentored Apollos (18:26–19:1) and sent him on to Corinth (where they had previously served) to encourage the believers there. They later also helped the church in Rome (Rom. 16:3) and risked their lives for Paul.

Ken was a lot like a young Timothy or a promising Aquila. He was a sales rep for a distributor of promotional and fund-raising materials for schools. He showed much potential but had some rough edges (like each of us). Ken had already begun to grow in a men's group when Greg, the leader, got hold of him. They began to run together each morning and built a solid friendship. Over time that friendship provided the environment for intentional discipleship and growth. Soon Ken was an apprentice leader. I (Bill) met him when he was in the process of becoming a full-fledged leader. After several more months of having Greg and me come alongside him, Ken became a leader of a men's group in my coaching huddle. He later became a coach and now leads and disciples men in a church in California, where he moved two years ago. Ken is the classic case of someone who grows into leadership through relationships of care and intentional development.

The care component comes into play right from the start. In any deepening relationship, your sole agenda is to get to know each other thoroughly. Leaders and apprentices should connect between meetings, spend time on the phone, and discuss next steps for development. This is true for group members as well. Time together outside of meetings will strengthen relationships and provide the trust needed to take group meetings to a new level. To raise the level of caring, you must also explore increasing levels of vulnerability. Every deep relationship involves risk before the fruit of development can be seen. This begins with knowing and being known, understanding one another's stories of spiritual journey with God.

Assess Needs for Growth

We each have our own version of how to assess the opportunities for growth. Some categorize needs as physical, emotional, and spiritual. Others seek to develop people in the areas of heart, soul, mind, and strength. It really doesn't matter, as long as a holistic approach is taken. We are complex, multifaceted beings. Shepherds care for and develop the whole sheep, not just one aspect.

The plan may vary based on how a leader or apprentice can invest in someone's life. So we encourage you to involve the entire group in the process, if possible, and allow the gifts of group members to shape one another. The member with an evangelism gift can influence those needing increased boldness in sharing their faith. The member with the gift of mercy will provoke everyone to have softer hearts toward those experiencing pain or loss.

Develop a Plan Together

The essential action in developing a plan for any member of the group focuses on identifying possible next steps, not on crafting a developmental plan for the next three decades. As you express love for group members and express genuine concern for their growth, they will contribute ideas for their own personal development.

Jot down a few objectives together. It may involve prayer, reading, or attendance at some event or worship service. Or it may involve steps to build a new relationship or bring fresh energy to an old relationship. In the end, a written plan with some next steps will foster clarity, create accountability, and allow progress to be measured. We will sometimes use a shepherding plan or a journal in which we list mutual objectives and prayer requests. When meeting with rising leaders, we refer to the plan for checking an individual's progress and seizing other new opportunities for growth.

Monitor Progress

As leaders continue building authentic, caring relationships with apprentices and group members, it will be easier to provide them with constructive and loving feedback. Together you can assess where additional care or discipleship is needed. Monitoring progress will allow you to affirm the growth of Christ followers and to point out new opportunities. You will soon find great joy and excitement as you fulfill the biblical injunction to "spur one another on toward love and good deeds" (Heb. 10:24).

I (Bill) have observed this firsthand in a number of groups—especially mine! Recently, as we renewed our group commitment and refined our covenant, I could see that members were wrestling with the care-discipleship tension and were striving to strike a balance. What resulted was a resounding commitment to spiritual growth and prayer but also the desire to create a safe, authentic, caring community. Right before my eyes was a group of men — executives, teachers, a doctor, a lawyer, a strategic planner, a trainer, and a pastor — insisting that we extend mutual care to one another! But at the same time, they also insisted that we strive to leverage that caring, loving environment for intentional spiritual growth in prayer, study, and exhortation to good deeds.

Your plans will be works in progress, because you'll discover new needs and will want to modify your plans, keeping things current and productive. Thus, the intentional shepherding process becomes a dynamic and evolving process of development.

One reminder for the whole group: as each person's developmental needs come into focus, and the more open you are about them, your group will begin to experience the mutual development we mentioned earlier. In groups, we develop one another.

Leaders cannot and should not carry the entire burden. Maturing groups understand this, and members take increased responsibility for the group's growth and for their own progress. As Paul says, "speaking the truth in love, we will in all things grow up into him who is the Head, that is, Christ. From him the whole body, joined and held together by every supporting ligament, grows and builds itself up in love, *as each part does its work*" (Eph. 4:15–16, italics ours).

Each part. That means each person in the group, whose combination of gifts, abilities, experiences, and, yes, biases — toward care or discipleship — will maintain a dynamic tension that will allow shepherding to happen.

Now that we have faced the learning and development challenges, the relational challenge becomes more evident. When you pursue spiritual transformation in an intentional shepherding environment, you must foster relationships to stimulate ongoing growth and change. How do we help our group members deepen relationships that will open up the Holy Spirit's activity in their lives? That's what the next chapter, on the relational challenge, tackles head-on. So keep your walking shoes on. The relational challenge requires great skill and promises rich rewards.

CHAPTER THREE

i'd like to get to know you . . . i think

MEETING THE RELATIONAL CHALLENGE BY BALANCING FRIENDSHIP AND ACCOUNTABILITY

How many people in your small group have "refrigerator rights"? According to therapist Will Miller and communications professor Glenn Sparks, the refrigerator may contain a clue about the level and quality of relationships in your life. Here's a test proposed by these two authors: "Imagine I come to your home for a first-time visit. We've never met before. You have invited me into your kitchen, and we are sitting at the table getting acquainted. Now suppose I get up, open your refrigerator, pull out the makings for a sandwich and start putting them together."

Miller and Sparks contend that most folks would be annoyed or offended by such behavior. But then they offer a contrasting scenario: "Let's say I'm your brother and come home for a visit. While we're catching up on the news, I get up, open your refrigerator and grab a cold soda. Are you upset? Of course not. Simply put, strangers don't have refrigerator rights; people really close to us do."[1]

Seeking Solid Relationships

The question of refrigerator rights gets at the heart of the small group relational challenge. Some members have experienced too little true friendship. Perhaps they've resigned themselves to casual connections and hardly dare hope for a little help from friends. Others may have been pressured by relationships that felt far too up close and personal. Good small groups find ways to build friendships they can count on.

Friend or Taskmaster?

Miller and Sparks report that about 44 million Americans move in any given year, roughly 17 percent of the population.[2] The authors also observe that most disorders treated by therapists are relational in nature, including anxiety, social detachment, and depression. Because people move so frequently, extended families are no longer part of most people's daily or weekly relational networks. It also means most people have fewer quality friendships, which usually take years to build. Families shy away from investing in relationships they will have to walk away from at the next departure. As a result, people must rely on their immediate family — including their kids — to fulfill many relational and emotional needs. This causes stress in marriages and places undue pressures on kids. Emotional problems often result from these relational voids.

Lack of solid relationships may also contribute to physical problems. It has been known for over a decade now that social ties reduce the risk of disease by lowering heart rate, blood pressure, and cholesterol. The well-known Harvard Medical School Nurses Health Study reported that those who had the most friends over a nine-year period cut their risk of early death by 60 percent. In fact, it was determined that not having a close friend or confidante was as detrimental to someone's health as smoking or being overweight.

So if it makes so much sense to have close friends, what's the problem? Why don't more people invest in relationships? Perhaps they never got a good look at a real friendship. Or maybe they experienced relationships that were close but choked with responsibility—absolutely no fun.

I (Bill) can't remember the exact words or even the name of the movie, but I vividly recall the scene: army boot camp. A shaggy assortment of new recruits steps off the bus and is greeted by their drill instructor (DI) for the first time. You know the speech: "Well, boys, we're gonna get to know each other *real* well for these next six weeks. We're gonna be pals—just you and me. Everywhere you turn, I'll be there. Every time you stop, I'll be in your face! When you stare in the mirror, I'll be lookin' back. I have just become your one and only friend. I'll be the first face you see in the morning and the last one you'll see at night! And if you have a bad dream, I'll be in it! Ain't gonna be no momma or poppa standing over your bed! I'm your momma and poppa. Am I making myself clear?" *Too clear.* Red, smiling faces turn pale gray and eager expressions fade to that deer-in-the-headlights look.

"This is the prettiest face you'll see for the next fifty days. Just me! And I am gonna turn you lazy sluggards into a lean, mean, fighting machine. When I give an order, you holler, 'Yes, sir!' When I say jump, you shout, 'How high, sir?' I'll be on your back every waking moment; I will push you harder and farther than you have ever gone.

And someday, when you are pinned down by mortar fire in some jungle halfway around the world, you'll thank me. But until then, remember: You can't run and you can't hide. You can't breathe without me knowing it. You can't move without me seeing it. You can't sneeze without me hearing it. I own you for the next six weeks, so get used to it. That's right; we're gonna be *real* good friends, you and me." *With friends like this, who needs enemies?*

In the military, the workplace, and sports, men and women alike encounter relationships characterized by high accountability. Though sometimes extreme, this accountability is generally healthy and beneficial. People need accountability in order to grow and be stretched, to fulfill responsibilities and meet new challenges. But a relationship heavy on accountability won't last if there is never any fun. Just ask how many soldiers became best friends with their DI at boot camp. Respect, maybe. Friendship? Not likely.

So which do you expect in a small group, friendship or accountability? If your relational life has been filled with DI types or bosses peering over your shoulder, you might avoid accountability in relationships. (I remember a college football player on a Top 20 team saying that the only time he felt any freedom on campus was when he was in the shower! It was the only place he could hide.) You just want some safe friends—people who make few demands and are fun to be with. People who laugh at your jokes and invite you over for the Super Bowl party.

Or you might be eager for more accountability, because your friendships have been built on convenience, comfort, and camaraderie. You have lots of fun playing ball together, carpooling, borrowing lawn mowers, or sharing recipes across the backyard. Folks may bring over brownies for a party or provide food when you are sick. Many people don't even get that far in their relational network. But relationships built only on convenience and casual connection fall short of true community. There must be more to a relationship for real growth and maturity in Christ to result.

Getting to Know You

What we really want is to bring accountability and friendship together somehow. The relational challenge we face can be characterized by the continuum below.

Friendship is a great thing. You might say it is the magnet that pulls people into groups. Pursuing friendship can help us break through barriers to true community. The quest for friendship is a spiritual quest, as Abraham's story shows. "And the scripture was fulfilled that says, 'Abraham believed God, and it was credited to him as righteousness,' and he was called God's friend" (James 2:23). Wow! Friendship with the Creator! We sometimes turn the business of being righteous into something deep and theological, but in the end it's about being God's friend.

Jesus called his disciples — his little community — together and said, "I no longer call you servants, because a servant does not know his master's business. Instead, I have called you friends, for everything that I learned from my Father I have made known to you" (John 15:15). "Friends" was the endearing term Jesus chose to describe those in the unique, growing relationship that had come to characterize his little community.

On the one end of the continuum is this wonderful gift of friendship. But the Bible warns of the peril of keeping things too casual for too long. "A man of many companions may come to ruin, but there is a friend who sticks closer than a brother" (Prov. 18:24). When you step back from church life to figure out how to move from "many companions" status to "a friend who sticks close," odds are it will be in a small group.

Proverbs also describes the accountability end of the relational tightrope: "Iron sharpens iron, and one person sharpens the wits of another" (27:17 NRSV). Iron sharpening iron is a metaphor for what happens when brothers and sisters in Christ "spur one another on toward love and good deeds" (Heb. 10:24) in the trenches of life-on-life connection. This is where someone can look you in the eye, or even deeper, into your heart and soul, and express concern for your spiritual well-being.

Accountability, built on trust and in tandem with love, turns connection into community, moving people from surface friendships to authentic relationships. Questions of the heart move people from casual conversations toward rich relationships. Small groups follow questions such as "How are you doing?" or "What are you learning?" with "Are you growing? Are you willing to do what is necessary to change?"

As scary as those questions sound, accountability can be the glue that keeps people linked to each other. In other words, friendship draws us into a group, but unless someone is willing to challenge us and help us grow, most of us won't stick with the group.

Remember Wayne, the guy who introduced us to polarity management? He is in my (Bill's) small group. One day, when discussing the group covenant and expectations, Wayne said, "I need a well-lit group." Everyone looked puzzled and asked, "What does that mean?"

He said, "It's a place where we can shine the light of truth on what is happening in our lives and hold each other accountable to some growth there. But it demands we become a safe place."

He was saying, "Let's build a friendship where there's trust, and then let's leverage that friendship for the purpose of accountability." He wanted our group to walk the tightrope, striving for that point of balance that produces authentic relationship. It looks like this:

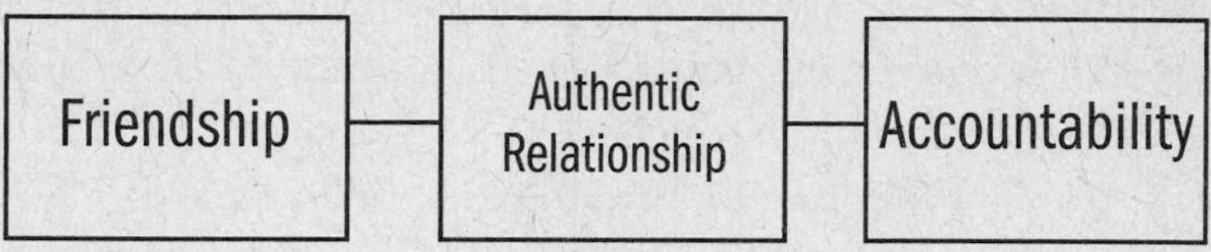

Deepening friendships must intentionally bring increasing accountability to the relationship. At the beginning of last year, I explained to our group how I wanted to break new ground and go deeper in my prayer life. I said, "I need you to hold me accountable. I have tried to do this alone. I keep making commitments and drifting back. I need you guys to look at me and ask, 'How's that going? What can we do to help?'"

But I don't want accountability to become the characteristic that defines my close relationships, even in my little community. I don't want people to walk into my group every week and say, "Okay, how's it going? Are you praying as much as you wanted? Did you pray this week? Today?" If you get such questions every time, you'll feel like your small group friends are spiritual drill instructors in training. You'll want to say, "Hey, do you play golf or anything? Do you ever smile or laugh?"

Excessive accountability throws a wrench into any small group's gear system. Too much accountability brings friendship building to a grinding halt. And too many superficial friendships will drain the desire for growth from members who long to be challenged and known in deep, caring ways. We need to find a balance between the two extremes.

So far in this book, we have faced the learning challenge, in which we must pursue spiritual transformation by managing the truth-life continuum. Then we wrestled with the development challenge, looking at how a leader can walk the tightrope between discipleship and care. As we confront the relational challenge—and every small group must—we focus on understanding the role members play in each other's lives, so that "each part does its work" (Eph. 4:16).

First Steps toward Authentic Relationship

How do we create authentic relationship? Where do you start in building a well-lit group? You'll find initial answers in *Building a Church of Small Groups*, in which we compiled guidelines from several sources, including Henri Nouwen, Bill Hybels, and John Ortberg.[3] Here's a brief overview.

- *To know and be known.* This happens when your group begins to get acquainted, so that each person's story is told and known. It is the beginning point for friendship and will provide the basis for accountability when people open up more of their lives to each other.
- *To love and be loved.* Small groups begin moving toward authentic relationship when members encounter their first moments of relational discomfort, when they find out things they don't like about another person but choose to love them anyway.

- *To serve and be served.* A litmus test of "groupness" is how the group responds in a crisis or time of need. Are people willing to serve another member when life turns against him or her? You will find out during difficulties. And will that serving mind-set become a group trademark?
- *To admonish and be admonished.* Speaking tough truth in love, or delivering a rebuke, is hard to do. It is scary and awkward. But it is a necessary component of relational authenticity.
- *To celebrate and be celebrated.* Celebrate what God is doing in your group, both for individual members and for the group as a whole. Take time to point out these spiritual victories.

Pursuing these five practices will place you on the path toward authentic relationship. But each practice has a gateway that every group member must pass through. For example, to walk the path of real knowing, you must enter through the gateway of self-disclosure. When a group walks through each gateway, it will find an ever-widening path toward real, lasting relationships.

Gateway 1: Self-Disclosure

Self-disclosure is the key that unlocks the door to community building. If vulnerability doesn't emerge with increasing frequency, you can't love, serve, admonish, or celebrate one another in community.

It's difficult to admonish a casual acquaintance or to be admonished by a stranger. When someone looks you in the eye and says, "You can do better. You made a promise to your kids and you are pulling back from it," you are at a crossroads. Without adequate self-disclosure, you will think, *Who are you? You hardly know me!* Self-disclosure gives us the right — earns us the right — to speak truth into each other's lives. Here are ways to promote self-disclosure in groups.

Relational Risk Taking

Self-disclosure means taking the risk of telling secrets. Has your group found it safe enough to finally take the first step of telling secrets, with members disclosing to the group something they've never told anybody else? That's a sure sign that vulnerability has gone to a new level.

Ken, a friend who always pushes the edge of spiritual growth, has been a role model of self-disclosure. He once said in his men's group, "If we are not going to talk about our struggles with sexual purity and encourage each other in times of temptation, I don't know if I can be part of this group. I need to talk about my struggles here and know that I am loved, supported, and held accountable. I confess this is a hard area, and I need some guys to walk with me." It was as though a cloud had been lifted from the room. One man after the other also shared how hard it was to keep pure thoughts and actions, especially in a culture mired in sexual exploitation and deviation. As a result, deeper friendships ensued, characterized by safety and truth telling.

Confidentiality

A small group can provide people with a safe environment that allows them to unlock their secrets. In a community built on confidentiality, members may share shocking secrets, ones not even their families know. In the example above, the group agreed to provide a safe place to talk about hard issues, fears, concerns, failings, and weakness. A key group guideline: what we talk about in the group stays in the group, unless permission is granted otherwise.

Icebreakers

Many people mistakenly think that icebreakers are a dispensable part of a small group meeting. Think again. These creative questions or activities can relieve or create tension. They can expose emotions, promote involvement, or open hearts and minds to deeper truth from Scripture. But you can never predict what will happen.

"What is one thing you're afraid you'll miss out on before your life ends?" was the question posed by the leader of a mixed group of couples and singles. A single woman broke the brief silence. "Sex," she blurted. Another moment of silence was broken by hysterical laughter that just wouldn't quit. The laughter relieved some tension for members shocked by her answer. But the icebreaker actually tripped issues the group could discuss, mainly about how a mixed group builds community. At what level do we share concerns? How do singles and married folks view the same issues? While nobody could believe she said it, the icebreaker provided the stage for self-disclosure and prompted a discussion about how a mixed group could work.

Icebreakers often elicit self-description — information that communicates "Here are some headlines about me and my life." But over time, as questions are asked and people take relational risks in a safe environment, self-description gives way to self-disclosure, where hearts are open and we unpack the real truth about one another.

Storytelling

In regular meetings and impromptu gatherings with group members, encourage people to share their stories with each other. Get them to talk about their faith journeys, their family backgrounds, places they have lived, and jobs they have held. In one group someone asked, "What was the strangest or most peculiar job you ever held?" The stories just flowed. Marketing executives had been barbers, a communications specialist had been a waiter in a chic restaurant, and an administrative assistant had been a soda jerk (at a diner in the 1950s), making malts and milkshakes for teens after high school.

Time

Let's just state the reality: the opportunity for self-disclosure increases with the amount of time you spend with one another. We advocate an extended time for gathering at least eight to twelve times a year, with an overnight retreat thrown in once or twice a year. Gathering around food, including families (for groups where that is not the norm), and having some fun will encourage relationship building and lower people's guards. If you meet weekly as a small group for less than ninety minutes and have no connections between group meetings, self-disclosure may come slowly. By adding extended gatherings and by connecting between group meetings in one-on-one settings or with each other's families, you can increase the level of self-disclosure.

Self-disclosure is the first gateway to building friendship *and* accountability. It will open up the second gateway to the relational tightrope.

Gateway 2: Acceptance and Belief

As the gateway to knowing and being known is self-disclosure, the gateway to loving and being loved is acceptance and belief. Just before I (Russ) finished my recent season of ministry at Willow Creek, I found myself in an interaction in which providing acceptance and belief took a relationship dramatically beyond where it had been. The discussion skimmed the surface through most of our lunch, but then the conversation took a defining turn.

"Can I ask you about something?" my friend asked, with a look that revealed this might be a dangerous question. "Sure," I replied, and then held my breath, wondering if I was about to be confronted or challenged.

"I was exploring a new ministry opportunity for me at the church," he said. *Whew, it was about him, not me!* He gave details of how the new ministry would involve working closely with a key leadership team at Willow Creek, substantially increasing his visibility and impact. And then my friend described a conversation with a member of that leadership team.

"As we discussed the broader exposure I would have at church, the team member expressed doubt about me having the position, worrying that I was seeking the new role because it would make others think more highly of me." He paused. Tears began to well up. "That was so hard to hear. Do you see that in me, too?"

Gulp. How do you respond to that? Especially when the observation was accurate. I quickly prayed for wisdom. (I'm not usually inclined to do that. I just didn't know what else to do and was buying as much time as I could!)

A long uncomfortable silence ensued, creating one of those awkward moments when it feels like there is no good thing to say. As I now look back, my next words must have been from the Holy Spirit. You know how every once in a while you sense God has taken over the communication? I know this is what happened, because I'm rarely as tender as I was with this man.

I began slowly. "Well, first let me say that I'm sorry you had to hear what you did in such a harsh way. It seems like that is part of the hurt you're now experiencing."

After his begrudging nod, I was bold enough to deliver the punch line.

"Even though the words were a bit harsh and direct, I think there is some truth in the observation," I said.

"Really?"

"Yes, really." More tears. More silence. It is painful when self-disclosure shows our dark side and friends are honest enough to affirm it. I knew my words would only deepen the wound, so I needed God to give me a gracious follow-up to the hard truth I had just expressed.

The next thought came to me through what felt like a pipeline from heaven. "I have one more thing to say when you're ready." A moment or two later, a nod gave the permission to move on. "Even though this is true about you right now, I will love you even if it never changes."

As those words emerged from the unlikely source of my lips, I saw in my friend's eyes a connection we'd never had. By God's grace, I had learned what it means to give someone the gift of acceptance and belief—accepting him for where he is today and believing in him for what he can become.

Acceptance goes one step beyond basic friendship by communicating "Even though this is true, *and even if this never changes,* I will still be with you. I will stay in the sphere of your community and remain your friend." That's true acceptance.

Belief then says, "If this is true, and even if this is something everybody else believes will never change, *I will still believe that it is possible for you to change.* I will stay by your side while we wait together for the Holy Spirit to work. I will be your defender and champion despite what others say or think."

The power of acceptance and belief to build authentic relationship is remarkable. And it must take up residence in the heart's inner room for group members to love and be loved as Christ would desire.

Gateway 3: Mutual Support

Community building may reach its zenith when crisis strikes. That's right—*when,* not *if*. It's only a matter of time before someone in the group collides head-on with life. Jesus was very frank about this reality of *when*. In John 16 he talks to his little community about his imminent suffering and death and then speaks words as realistic as any he taught: "In this world you will have trouble. But take heart! I have overcome the world" (v. 33). A truism says that two things are certain in the world: death and taxes. There is a third: trouble. And true communities serve one another, especially in times of trouble. Unfortunately, not all groups pass the test.

Look at the small group led by Jesus himself. His group not only abandons him, but one member betrays him and another denies knowing him by profaning his name. The ones the Messiah called "friends" failed the crisis test of community.

But crisis can be very effective in providing an opening to true community. The weak, needy, or broken among us present our groups with opportunities for real growth. To enjoy relationship only with the strong and healthy provides a false sense of community. "The elimination of the weak is the death of the fellowship," said Dietrich Bonhoeffer. In fact, when a group rallies together to meet the needs of a struggling member, it creates a spiritual openness that unlocks the door to friendship and accountability.

Lynn and I (Russ) will never forget the people who helped us after our house burned down in 1999. Those who walked closest with us grew in their friendship with us, because these friendships were proven in the darkest hour of our lives. These people earned the right to provoke hard but essential conversations about what we were learning through adversity. Their service in crisis opened the door for mutual accountability. By contrast, friends who remained relationally distant had little right or ability to speak into our lives at that point. Mutual support and care built both ends of the relational continuum — enduring friendships and accountability.

But there is one caveat: service must be mutual in true community. We cannot allow some members to always be givers and some to always be takers. What if we never reciprocated when others met hardship? Obviously, that would be a community breaker. The gateway to authentic relationship is *mutual* support and willingness to meet needs.

Humility is the product of mutual support and service. As people serve and are served, a gracious and humble environment is created. And then a wonderful thing begins to happen: people don't wait for a crisis in order to serve. They begin to anticipate needs and seek opportunities to help others in the group.

My (Bill) family is part of an intergenerational group in our church. It consists of one couple, four singles, and four families with kids. Our group has no problem serving in a crisis. But recently we watched members serve out of pure humility and joy. At one meeting we each described talents God has given us — writing, teaching, music, art, woodworking. One woman remarked, "I love to make special gifts and creative artifacts out of wood, also, but have not been able to for years. These projects are made with a scroll saw, and we can't afford to have one. But someday, when we can put the money together, I'd love to have one and make things for people."

Her comments were authentic and heartfelt, without any sense of complaint or discontent. Many of us were aware of her family's challenging financial situation, so several members of the group secretly solicited donations for this special table saw. It was fun to watch them present it to her as a gift a few weeks later. Talk about joy and gratitude, humility and love, all rolled into one emotive celebration! Wow! To serve the family in this way signaled, "You matter to us — in times of crisis and just because we love you!"

Gateway 4: Truth Telling

Sheryl Fleisher leads the internship program at Willow Creek and formerly led our single adult ministry. One of the best people-developers we've ever seen, Sheryl described a formative small group experience one day when she was teaching leaders.

"When I was sixteen years old," she began, "I got the opportunity to experience what I would call my first, real Acts 2 small group. We were high school juniors, and Paula was our leader. She began to spend personal time with each one of us, building relationships and fostering spiritual growth. After about six months, one day she sat me down and said, 'Sheryl, it's time for us to have a heart-to-heart talk.' I said, 'Alright.' And Paula very lovingly, but very directly and bluntly, said to me, 'Sheryl, I think you're a fake. I've watched you in the group for six months and I've watched you on Sundays. You say all the right things and you do all the right things. But I watch you during the week as well, and I don't see the love of God, the joy of God, and the peace of God flowing out of your life. There's something wrong, Sheryl. I think you're faking it.'

"And she was right. She had gotten close enough to me to see through the surface, to know and love me. And that was the turning point in my life. It was the first time I think I became vulnerable, broken, and honest before God, Paula, and myself! I confessed, 'God, I don't want to play games anymore. I don't want to play church. I don't want to play Christianity. I give you my mind, my will, my heart, my body. I'm all yours, God. Whatever you want to do, I'm yours.'"

One of the greatest gifts you'll give the people in your group is the truth—the truth about God, about the world, and about who they really are. Once they're known and loved and feel safe in the relationship, you can speak gracious and transforming words of truth into their lives.

That's what admonition is. It's saying to someone, "Would you be open to an observation I have about your life?"

Admonition is not about resolving conflict in a relationship. (We'll talk about that in the next chapter.) Rather, it's about urging another person to clean up their act and get back on track with God. To admonish is to correct or rebuke and is used in a relationship to point out destructive behaviors or attitudes. It also serves to push someone to a next step in spiritual growth that they have been avoiding or neglecting. "I have a challenge for you if you're open to it sometime."

The biblical roots of this activity are found in 2 Timothy 4:2: "correct, rebuke and encourage—with great patience and careful instruction." These words to Timothy are set in the context of Paul's exhortation to teach biblical truth. Admonition not rooted in truth feels like criticism or faultfinding. To both correct and encourage, admonition must be shared with grace, tact, and emotional intelligence. Most of us lack the great patience required for careful instruction. More often than not, we'll come across as pontifical know-it-alls, and those in our little community will feel the edge of rebuke more than the motivation we want to give them.

That's because we are more interested in how their behavior affects us than them. To become wise in correcting, rebuking, and encouraging, we must check our motives.

Paul's "careful instruction" mandate is a good one, too. It requires us to offer more than two-bit answers to million-dollar issues. If we hope to help someone, we must offer something worthwhile and carefully considered. The result will be spiritual growth. Thus Paul teaches, "Instead, speaking the truth in love, we will in all things grow up into him who is the Head, that is, Christ" (Eph. 4:15).

Gateway 5: Affirmation

As a group passes through each of the prior gateways, many opportunities will open up for the work of affirmation. The best explanation of the principle of affirmation comes from the great theologian Thumper, of *Bambi* fame. Quoting his mom, Thumper the rabbit said, "If you can't say anything nice, don't say anything at all." Or as we might paraphrase it for our purposes here, "Be on the lookout for nice things to say" (NBRV — the New Bill and Russ version of *Bambi*).

Of course, the Thumper principle is just a mildly entertaining version of what the Bible has always told us in Ephesians 4:29: "Do not let any unwholesome talk come out of your mouths, but only what is helpful for building others up according to their needs, that it may benefit those who listen."

Easy to quote, hard to do. Communities tend to migrate toward well-meaning banter, humor, and idle discussion. We all know how humor or mild teasing can open up relational connections in light but wonderful ways. But sometimes an ill-timed laugh can cover wounds and raise defenses. We know it, because the two of us often lead the band when it comes to keeping fun in the mix.

Ephesians 4:29 teaches us to do more than avoid offensive speech; it suggests saying "*only* what is helpful." Yikes! Maybe we need to consider our words a little more soberly. Words of hope and affirmation will do more to build community than you can imagine.

The meaningfulness of affirmation can surprise the affirmers as much as the affirmed. A thirty-seven-year-old man came to faith through a small group. A few months after his conversion, the group discovered it was his birthday and brought a cake, sang to him, and showered him with affirmation. He broke down in tears, a response they had hardly expected. Then he gently reminded them of his background, and suddenly they understood. He was a Jehovah's Witness when he first encountered people from the group. The Witnesses don't celebrate people, and they don't do birthdays. This was his first experience of being celebrated and encouraged. Affirmation paves the way for meaningful celebration as a group accomplishes their mission and grows together in Christ.

Debbie, a group leader at First Alliance in Calgary, Alberta, wrote to us about the power of celebration in a group. The group of fourteen had experienced great growth and community in over three years of meeting. They decided to birth into two new groups so that more people could experience life-giving community. Here are her own words:

After dinner we gathered in the family room, where we were presented with a rock and a marker. We each wrote a word or two on our rock about what the group had meant to us and why it was so vital. There were lots of tears and laughs as we looked through our spiritual photo album and recalled everything God had done among us. The rocks were then placed in the middle of the room, becoming a kind of altar — an altar of remembrance.

Then we had communion together and Larry, our leader, told each of us what he appreciated about us as he served us communion. There were tons of tears! It was a sweet time of community. Then the six of us gathered with Lorne, our apprentice leader, in the middle of the room while Larry and the rest prayed over us, commissioning our new group. Then we changed places and the six prayed for the eight.

The evening ended with balloons and a birthday cake. It had a profound effect on everyone. It was God honoring and, although we were sad to birth, we knew it was right. We are all very excited to see whom God will send our way!

Affirming each other in the context of community will do more to build friendship than you might imagine, and it will take the edge off accountability, because group members will know you are *for* each other, first and foremost. Don't ever underestimate the power a small group has to give a blessing to people — to celebrate what God has done in their lives.

Lead the Way

Self-disclosure, acceptance, mutual support, truth telling, and affirmation will put your small group on the path toward authentic relationship. But here's the bottom line with these five gateway truths: continuing together along this path requires that the leader lead the way. It's up to you to find comfortable ways for your members to build friendship and accountability.

True leadership brings us right back to the first gateway. If you want your group members to risk being known, you must be vulnerable enough to practice self-disclosure.

I had a poignant reminder of this in a couples' group Lynn and I (Russ) led last year. The group had been together about six months, and I could feel a little relational stagnation setting in, so I decided to push. We were using a curriculum with more questions than we could typically answer in one meeting, so I would choose about one-third of the questions for our discussions. This time I cherry-picked one question that I thought might cause us to reveal things we'd never talked about in our small group. It was a risky question that would take us beyond information to deeper vulnerability, if our group members would bite the bait.

I asked the question, and it got really quiet—as I had expected it would. Things were going as I had planned; I knew the group was being challenged at a new level. But suddenly a woman in the group caught me off guard. She said, "I think you should answer that question first."

After stammering and wondering how to dodge her challenge, a thought came to me. I smiled, looked at her, and said, "You know what I have in my mind right now? I have this picture." I went on to describe the friendship-accountability tightrope, explaining how authentic relationship is formed by self-disclosure, and how the leader has to lead the way. So I did.

I had to lead the way that day. I had to answer first if I really wanted us to grow in our self-disclosure. If you are a small group leader, you will have to lead the way as well. You'll have to initiate friendships and invite accountability. You will need to practice, as best you can, self-disclosure, acceptance and belief, mutual support, truth telling, and consistent affirmation. It's going to happen in your group because you lead the way. Groups don't just stumble into relational authenticity.

Focus on Friendship

Now, what if you're light on the friendship side of the continuum? Well, the best time to build friendships is between meetings. Groups tend to think about the next meeting, not how to weave the group's relational fabric into the interim. There are 168 hours in a week. After eating, sleeping, and working, (and *Monday Night Football*), there are still about 40 to 50 hours in which to connect as members. Those hours provide powerful opportunities to foster authentic relationships.

You can seize planned and unplanned moments. Schedule friends for dinner or a walk, invite a group member on an errand, drop in for coffee, or get the kids together. Task-based groups should schedule time away from the task to develop a deeper relational network. Designate one night as "drop by" night at the house. "Anyone can come anytime. We'll have some hot cider and snacks, and a few games to play. Bring kids if you have 'em. We'll be here." The side conversations and impromptu moments may be remarkably transforming.

We also recommend scheduling a group retreat. The extended time away from work and home allows you to get to know one another and reveals new sides of your fellow group members.

Create Comfortable Accountability

Comfortable accountability? Sounds like an oxymoron, doesn't it? But if you are walking the tightrope well, the friendship end of the continuum will make accountability more comfortable. There are two ways to help create comfortable accountability.

If you're too light on the accountability side, encourage people toward church membership — what we at Willow Creek call *participating membership.* When people take steps to seriously commit to the local church, they tend to evaluate how they're doing spiritually. Accountability is a natural by-product as you guide your group toward seeking God's purposes through local church commitment.

Leaders can use the membership discussion to prompt group members to take responsibility for pursuing growth. This accountability conversation helps a group refine its covenant and gain clarity about why the group exists. We ask, "Are we growing together as part of the local church, or are we simply creating our own little spiritual haven? To whom are we accountable as a group, and how do we serve the local community?" These are great questions that deserve time and attention.

A second way to foster accountability is to focus on certain individuals in the group. I (Bill) meet personally with members from my group, which helps me to learn more about individual needs and spot opportunities for growth, service, or leadership. Our whole group utilizes this practice with one another, and the quality and depth of accountability have plummeted. While mutual support is the aim, at times a person will feel safest revealing something to a leader first. Later, the person can express his or her need for accountability to the group, which will in turn encourage others to do the same.

As you meet the relational challenge with fervor and courage, and as authentic relationship grows to deeper levels of friendship and accountability, people are bound to step on a few interpersonal land mines. Tensions will arise and the group will encounter conflict — as a whole or between members. When this happens — and it will — how will you reconcile relational breakdown in your little community? How will you meet the reconciliation challenge? Turn the page and learn the skills of walking one of the most challenging and rewarding tightropes of all.

CHAPTER FOUR

how to have a good fight

MEETING THE RECONCILIATION CHALLENGE BY BALANCING KINDNESS AND CONFRONTATION

I thought this group was going to spend more time on Bible study," said Kim.

"Frankly, I get enough Bible personally and from a class I am taking," Mike responded. "What we need in this group is some action. We should be focused on serving more."

"Wait a minute, Mike. If I wanted to be on a mission team, I would have signed up for one." Peter openly expressed his family's growing frustration. "We moved here eight months ago, and I'm still trying to connect with people and develop lasting friendships. I was hoping that might happen here."

"We can't just expect everyone in the group to be our best friends. I have several lifelong relationships and can't even keep up with the people I already know," said Sarah. "I need some accountability and a place to get to know God better! Sure, if I find a friend or two here, that's great. But I need to live life on the spiritual edge."

"Exactly," said Kim. "Which is why I wanted us to focus on Bible study. No truth, no change. I certainly don't want to be in a touchy-feely therapy group. My last small group was that way. I think it's time in this group that we get serious about growth."

"Who said I wasn't serious about growing?" Mike suspected Kim's subtle comment was directed at him. "You don't have to bow down to Bible study to be more like Christ."

Ouch, thought Tom, choosing not to step into the debate. This was the hottest this group had gotten in the four months he'd been leading it.

"I know what you mean. Our last church was filled with Bible experts," remarked Peter, now siding with Mike. "It was the coldest place we've ever worshiped. We lasted about four months before moving on. Those people were bibliolaters!"

Kim was about to blow her stack. She'd never been called a "Bible worshiper" before.

"Okay," she hissed, "why don't we just toss Scripture out the window and talk psychobabble to each other! So, Mike, are you getting in touch with your inner world? Are you in the process of becoming your real self? Maybe it's time for another visit to Dr. Phil."

Kristin, usually quiet and reserved, couldn't help but laugh. But Mike found no humor in the remark. It was easy to see that he and Peter were forming a team, while Kim and Sarah found sympathy with each other's views. It was time for Tom to lead — to step in and exercise his authority. But he was uncertain where to begin and how.

"It sounds like we all have some ideas about the group. Maybe we should pray and see what God wants us to do." *That should calm things down. No one ever argues about praying.* Unfortunately, Tom had underestimated the energy in the room.

"Excuse me, Tom, but spiritualizing this won't help the matter," said Peter. "I think Kim needs to apologize to Mike; that remark was way out of line."

"Oh, let's just forget all this arguing. It won't get us anywhere," offered Kristin, looking for an escape hatch. "Anyhow, it smells like the brownies are just about done." Kristin excused herself, saying she needed to check on the dessert the group had planned to eat after the meeting. But everyone knew she was trying to put a band-aid on a mortal wound.

"I wasn't trying to spiritualize anything," began Tom. "I just wanted ..."

"I don't think Kim is the problem here," interrupted Sarah, looking Mike straight in the eyes. She never would have spoken so boldly if Kristin, Mike's wife of two years, hadn't left the room. Sarah's remark surprised Mike, but he had no intention of apologizing. He believed he'd said nothing that warranted an apology. He sat motionless.

Dead silence. Tom's mind was spinning. *What do I do? How did we get here? In a few minutes we would have been laughing over coffee and dessert. Now we are in a big mess! I have never seen Kim so angry. And what's with Peter? For a guy that needs friends, he isn't making any points with the group. What in the world just happened?*

Conflicts Happen

My (Bill's) mother loved to joke with us when we were young, playing on our gullibility and egos. "You're perfect children," she'd say. Just as we began to gloat she'd add, "When you're asleep!" Small groups work perfectly, too — when no people join them, that is! And that is about the only time a group is perfect. Groups can be messy because people show up, and we're glad they do! But when people show up, there is always the potential for conflict. As a matter of fact, conflict is a normal part of group life. Pursuing relational integrity in an environment in which truth meets life will inevitably lead to relational friction. And when it happens, groups must embrace it. Though the Bible acknowledges how often Christians quarrel, it presents Christ's desire and prescription for unity. Even the greatest of biblical saints have slugged it out on the pages of Scripture.

Reality Check

In Galatians 2:11–14, the apostle Paul describes a showdown between two great church leaders, himself and Peter:

> When Peter came to Antioch, I opposed him to his face, because he was clearly in the wrong. Before certain men came from James, he used to eat with the Gentiles. But when they arrived, he began to draw back and separate himself from the Gentiles because he was afraid of those who belonged to the circumcision group. The other Jews joined him in his hypocrisy, so that by their hypocrisy even Barnabas was led astray.
>
> When I saw that they were not acting in line with the truth of the gospel, I said to Peter in front of them all, "You are a Jew, yet you live like a Gentile and not like a Jew. How is it, then, that you force Gentiles to follow Jewish customs?"

Using his confrontation with Peter as a backdrop, Paul exhorts the Galatians to act on one of the ramifications of the gospel, that Jew and Gentile believers are one in Christ because the cross obliterated the barriers between them. Peter—and the Galatian church—needed a reality check. And who better to give it than Paul, never known for his timidity or shyness! This is Paul at his confrontational best, eager to ultimately reconcile Peter with the community, Jews with Gentiles, sinners with God.

When experiencing conflict in our small groups, we begin not with our differences, but with God's design for relationships. We all want to reconcile our differences—but to what? What is the standard to which we call one another? When salvation and sanctification were at stake, Paul appealed to the core of the gospel, clarified again in Galatians 3:28 in case anyone missed it earlier in his letter. "There is neither Jew nor Greek, slave nor free, male nor female, for you are all one in Christ Jesus." Paul called Peter to align his practice with the truth of the gospel regarding salvation and sanctification. To what biblical standard or truth do we align community building in the face of conflict?

For our own alignment, we often return to Jesus' words in John 17:20–23: "My prayer is not for them alone. I pray also for those who will believe in me through their message, that all of them may be one, Father, just as you are in me and I am in you. May they also be in us so that the world may believe that you have sent me.... May they be brought to complete unity to let the world know that you sent me and have loved them even as you have loved me."[1]

Look at Jesus' desire for relationships in the body of Christ. First, observe the pattern. "Just as you are in me and I am in you." Now that's a standard for oneness! Jesus prays that his followers will relate in community the same way he and the Father interact. He asks that we model the oneness of the Trinity—not just any small group—the Trinity! Let that one sink in for a moment.

God is one but exists in three persons, Father, Son, and Spirit, and they've been together through all eternity. They experience community with incredible purity, joy, and delight. It is all this community has known, from all time. It is all they will ever know, for all time. It is the supreme community—relational love of another kind, not of this world.

It is the community of the Trinity that Jesus uses as his reference point while praying for his small group, the band of followers he has now called his friends in light of his imminent death. Twice in the prayer—in verses 20–23 and in verse 11—Jesus prays to his Father concerning the eleven disciples "that they may be one as we are one." It's a stunning prayer, considering the makeup of this diverse group of eleven (now without Judas).

Now, here is a small group leader's nightmare. Thomas the perennial skeptic, Peter the impulsive, and James and John, fighting for prominence at Jesus' side and wanting to call down fire on cities that rejected their message. Then there's quiet Bartholomew, Matthew the tax collector, Simon the Zealot, eager to overthrow the Roman authorities, and all the rest—each personality headed on a collision course with the others. Nevertheless, Jesus prayed, "that they may be one as we are one." He really believed it could happen, even in his little community of fragmented followers.

And he believes it can happen in your group too. "My prayer is not for them alone [the eleven disciples]. I pray for those who will believe in me through their message [that's us], that all of them may be one." Jesus had our relational unity in mind almost two thousand years ago!

It is the will of the Trinity, not that we should become like God, not that we should become gods, but that we should be invited into the fellowship of the Trinity. That may be the most remarkable phrase in all of Scripture. We have been invited into this eternal and most remarkable divine community of oneness.

God longs for us to join him in oneness, and to live that kind of life every day. But why is this so essential? Does God simply want us to enjoy great fellowship, to hang out in the fellowship hall of heaven over some angelic pastries and coffee? Hardly. Gilbert Bilezikian describes God's ultimate intent:

> Despite this almost embarrassingly repetitious insistence on oneness, Jesus went on praying, "that they may become completely one, so that the world may know that you have sent me." Just prior to his sacrifice on the cross, Jesus' heart ached for his followers to band together in communities that would reflect authentic oneness so that their witness to the world would be effective.
>
> This concern for the survival of the church down through the ages provides the explanation for the anguished tones of Jesus' prayer. He knew that if the church should fail to demonstrate community to the world, it would fail to accomplish its mission because the world would have reason to disbelieve the gospel (vv. 21, 23). According to that prayer, the most convincing proof of the gospel is the perceptible oneness of his followers.[2]

That is why meeting the reconciliation challenge is so important—and so difficult. It involves a spiritual battle for the souls of men and women who are far from God. And the greatest weapon in this battle is the oneness of the church. Oneness cannot be achieved if group members avoid conflict, live in pretense, and harbor resentment toward others. Christ prays for a reconciled community, one that is pure and true in Christ, boldly declaring the reality of his incarnation and demonstrating to the world that Jesus is still in the life-change business.

And he desires for others to find the community that he shares with the Father and the Spirit. Jesus' community is not a closed group. He wants his community to be extended to mere mortals. "May they also be in us." He wants it so badly that he was willing to go to the cross, to reconcile the world to himself. And so he opens his eternal fellowship to the likes of people like you and me.

The implications of this are mind-boggling. To tolerate disunity in the body of Christ is unthinkable. That's why the Scripture exhorts, "Make every effort to keep the unity of the Spirit through the bond of peace" (Eph. 4:3). We dare not damage or destroy the community into which we've been invited. We are called to participate in Trinitarian oneness here on earth in our little communities. We can never go back. Jesus' words changed everything: "May they be in us."

Kim and Mike Meet the Trinity

You will find dissonance in most relationships. It's only a matter of time till you feel pangs of the Fall, as others' resulting imperfections adversely affect your life. You will probably shrug off the lion's share and chalk it up to mood swings, personality quirks, "that's just the way they are," and the inevitability of people being people. *If only people in the group were less fallen, like me!* Often your feelings about it will remain subconscious; if you were to stop long enough to process every relational hiccup, nothing else would get done.

It is relatively easy for people to talk about truth and share about life. They can extend some measure of care and even help each other grow. It can be pretty simple for people to take their first steps toward deepening relationships. But soon they begin to rub up against each other — different personalities, different dreams about what the group should be about, different perspectives about the truth, even doctrinal disagreements. These disagreements will ultimately tap into the sin that separates us from one another if we cannot deal with it, as Kim and Mike discovered.

So the question is not whether a group will encounter breakdown, but how they will respond when it does. And once again, you will find responses that range along the entire continuum, requiring groups to walk the reconciliation tightrope. It looks like this:

On one end of the continuum are the people who operate mostly on the kindness. These people are epitomized by TV personalities like the fictitious army private Gomer Pyle, played by actor Jim Nabors. Gomer was the nicest guy you ever met, more like a young Boy Scout than a Marine Corps grunt. He helped old ladies across the street and wouldn't hurt a flea. If Gomer had been a small group leader, he'd have started a care group for hurting and lonely fleas—that's the kind of guy he was.

On the other end of the continuum are people who operate mostly through confrontation. Gomer Pyle's nemesis, Sergeant Carter, epitomizes the people on this end of the spectrum. He was always in everyone's face, especially Pyle's. Carter was conflict personified. Confrontation could have been his middle name. He didn't have a kind bone in his body and would grow melancholy when he didn't have a relational battle to fight. It was always just a matter of time before Pyle and Carter were going at it. Well, actually it was Carter going at it and Gomer smiling passively and taking it. The show epitomized kindness versus confrontation.

Some of you grew up after the Gomer Pyle era and are more familiar with Mr. Rogers and Mr. T. Every child's friend, Fred Rogers, hosted *Mister Rogers' Neighborhood.* In Mr. Rogers' neighborhood, it was always a beautiful day to be his neighbor. No one said no when Fred Rogers asked his audience of three- and four-year-olds each day, "Would you like to be my neighbor? Sure, I knew you would." Yep. Making friends was easy for Mr. Rogers. You could never imagine him in a confrontation with anyone, especially not with Mr. T.

Mr. T—the Herculean, Mohawk-wearing, chain-laden, rough-talking champion of *The A-Team*—was the 1980s poster child for confrontation. The renegade, soldiers-of-fortune A-Team thrived in the Los Angeles underground, a not so beautiful neighborhood. Mr. T played Sergeant Bosco "Bad Attitude" Baracus, whose life mission was to stomp out evil. Today Mr. T appears on the networks selling long-distance phone service, bringing his confrontational style into every commercial.

Mr. Rogers versus Mr. T—now there's a pair. Could they find a Trinitarian community of oneness? Or how about Mother Teresa and the Godfather (or Al Capone, or the Sopranos)? You get the idea. Your small group likely includes people at both ends of the kindness-confrontation continuum. They may not have the extreme personalities we just described. But you know your group members, so you know how they respond to tension or conflict in the group, with either kindness (an attempt to ease the pain) or head-on confrontation.

Both are biblical responses that a group must practice. Thus, we have another tightrope. Romans 2:4 says that God's "kindness leads you toward repentance." Kindness can lead people to face that which they otherwise won't face. It's a good thing.

Second Timothy 4:2 portrays the confrontation end, telling us that unless we "correct, rebuke and encourage — with great patience and careful instruction" — we can't bring people back into line to grow in truth. There are times when confrontation is necessary.

The Bible offers plenty of examples of kindness and confrontation. Jesus blesses Peter when he confesses that Jesus is the Messiah (Matt. 16:16–17) but nails him a few verses later for discounting the prediction of death and resurrection: "Get behind me, Satan!" (16:23). Paul "opposed him [Peter] to his face" (Gal. 2:11) but could also act like a doting mother, describing Timothy as "my true son in the faith" (1 Tim. 1:2) and advising Timothy to attend to his physical well-being (5:23).

God uses both means when dealing with sin. Sometimes he meets sinful people with gentleness: "Or do you show contempt for the riches of his kindness, tolerance and patience, not realizing that God's kindness leads you toward repentance?" (Rom. 2:4). But the next verses remind us that God will confront sin directly on "the day of God's wrath" and "give to each person according to what he has done" (Rom. 2:5–6).

In groups, both kindness and confrontation can be right responses. The challenge is to bring both together in healthy conflict — where kindness and confrontation meet.

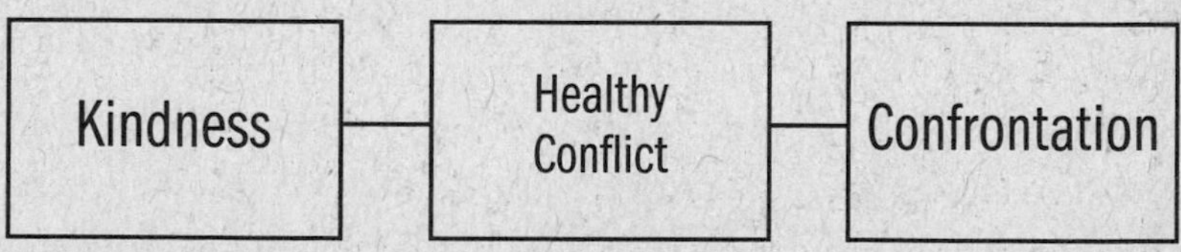

Healthy conflict seems like an oxymoron, but it's not. Healthy conflict occurs when people have enough heart, enough tenderness, but also a willingness to look someone in the eye and say, "We need to talk. We need to have a discussion." Healthy conflict can facilitate some of the most transforming moments your group will ever have.

Diagnosing Causes of Conflict

One of the best ways for a group to walk the reconciliation tightrope and engage in healthy conflict resolution is to recognize factors that contribute to the problem. Following are common factors that may lead to conflict in groups.

Group Stages

Groups, like people, move through developmental stages. The book *Leading Life-Changing Small Groups* described those stages as shown in the table on the following page.

As in marriage, groups begin at the honeymoon phase. Everyone loves each other and there are few problems. But after a few meetings, the glow fades. Within six to nine months, it is not uncommon for a group to experience conflict. Why? Because people have come to know each other.

Group members discover that they don't really have as much in common as they thought they did. They realize that affinity, often the beginning point for small group connection, contributes very little to the long-term relational health of true community. The balance of their value to each other will have to be earned over time.

When Gail and I (Bill) moved to Chicago, we led a couples' group that encountered group stages nearly by the book. At first we experienced a wonderful level of connection with other members. We would return home and remark, "What a God-thing! This is fabulous! How about the Johnsons [not their real name]? What a couple!"

Helping Group Members Process Growing Pains

Stage	Formation	Exploration	Transition	Action	Birthing	Termination
# Meetings Per Stage	4–6	6–10	4–8	12–24	4–8	2–6
Member's Questions	Who is in the group? Do I like my group?	Do I fit here? How is our group doing?	Are we really open with each other? Will this group accomplish its mission?	Authentic Relationship	Authentic Relationship	Authentic Relationship
Member's Feelings	Excitement Anticipation Awkwardness	Comfortable Relaxed Open	Tense Anxious Impatient Doubtful	Eager Open Vulnerable Supportive	Grief Enthusiasm Loss Anticipation Fear	Respectful Reflective Thankful Sad
Member's Role	Gather information about others	Give information Accept others	Provide feedback Express frustration	Express feelings Use my gifts Take ownership Accept challenges	Express concerns Accept reality Discuss changes Give blessing	Show love Express thanks Affirm relationships
Leader's Response	Caring Clear Accepting	Affirmation Feedback Warmth Modeling	Confront Encourage Challenge	Challenge Affirm Guide Release	Listen actively Acknowledge feelings Affirm members	Review Reflect Respond
Leader's Role	Communicate vision Promote sharing Define goals	Generate trust Discuss values Facilitate relationships Create covenant	Provide self-disclosure Re-examine covenant Be flexible	Provide service opportunities Clarify goals Begin seeking 2nd apprentice Celebrate results	Cast vision Pray for birth Create sub-groups Communicate with apprentice	Celebrate Give Gifts Communion Bring closure
Content of Communication	Events Topics Facts	Topics People Group God's nature	Personal thoughts Feelings Values God's plan	Group relationships Tasks God's work	People Leadership Vision God's desires	Relationships People God's blessings
Style of Communication	Responsive General Brief	Descriptive Social Explanatory	Assertive Argumentative Directive One-way	Speculative Cooperative Interactive Two-way Confrontive	Interactive Confrontive Expressive	Reflective Understanding Affirming

But after six or eight more meetings, we drove home thinking, "What's with the Johnsons? What is their problem? Should they really be in the group?" We had definitely moved past the honeymoon phase, when everyone is friendly and nice. Our initial thinking—that everyone was going to like each other all the time—soon gave way to reality.

There we were, talking about the Johnsons differently than in the first two meetings. We saw how they raised their kids and approached life and its problems. And we thought, "We would never do that!" So we started to build barriers.

Conflict is natural as a group progresses through various growth stages. (Think about how kids navigate adolescence and the concurrent hormonal changes!) Just as in marriage, conflict reoccurs. As a group moves through each phase, things can get a little bumpy. Conflict comes in cycles, so be prepared.

You can use the above chart as a community GPS (global positioning system) to find out what is normal as small groups experience natural stages of their growth. Having confirmed that an experience is routine, you can reassure your group with words like, "What we're experiencing is pretty predictable; we're just trying to figure out if we like each other and want to stay together for the long haul." It can help relieve the conflict.

Conflict will arise as your group moves from friendship toward accountability. Getting in each other's faces a little challenges the group's comfort zone. Everyone must adjust and reengage at new levels of intimacy and authenticity. Being aware of group stages will help you calm each other.

Relational Unawareness

Sometimes conflict arises because your group has somebody best described as a *relationally unaware* person. Everyone has some measure of relational immaturity, so every group member will contribute a certain degree of unawareness. But the group and, in particular, the leader, must confront extreme unawareness.

I (Russ) experienced this once on a small group visit, which I do from time to time despite overseeing the whole small group ministry. The group had invited me to visit them, and I knew the leader pretty well. It seemed like a good chance to dig a little deeper into our ministry to see how things really were on the front lines of community.

It only took a few minutes to see that this group had a problem. One member was more relationally unaware than anyone I had ever seen in a small group. The group responded to it all right (expressing some kindness), and the leader was managing the dynamic quite well (beginning some confrontation). But I left that meeting sensing that unless the behavior was confronted, existing members would soon tire of the situation, and prospective members would lose interest in joining.

It's difficult when someone talks too much or practices excessive self-disclosure, which can be embarrassing for the group. How do you respond to this kind of careless speech? Visualizing the kindness-confrontation continuum may help. Most likely you will need to move toward the confrontational end. You will probably begin by confronting the person privately, kindly helping them understand their impact on the group dynamics. (The appendix describes the process for confronting someone in love and speaking truth during relational breakdown.)

Small groups provide excellent opportunities to handle such socialization issues. It's not that these people are bad; they're just relationally unaware. Perhaps they've never had opportunities to develop interpersonal skills or overcome unhealthy models of relating. In any case, change is possible, and groups can function in healthy ways *if the problem is honestly addressed.*

Extra Care Required

Occasionally someone in your group will require more attention and care than the average member does. This condition may result from a crisis or an illness and may be temporary or become chronic. Being in Extra Care Required (ECR) territory is not good or bad; it simply reflects reality. Your group can handle a lot of ECR situations if you remember to navigate the tension between kindness and confrontation.

When my (Russ) family lost our home to a fire, I became our group's ECR person for a few months. Our small group had to come alongside me and mete out extra kindness and support. That's just common sense.

Most extra care situations are seasonal, lasting a short time until the situation is under control or has been adequately addressed. But what if the situation becomes chronic? When a person has long-term ECR needs, you should begin to move carefully from kindness to confrontation. To be clear, you should not drop or ignore kindness; you simply begin to bring the confrontation component of healthy conflict into play. Lest you think we lack mercy, don't stop reading. This is where you will learn to provide kindness and care without placing excessive demands on the leader or the group — and that is a good thing!

Begin by setting boundaries for ECR people. Help them understand what the group can and *cannot* do for them. Unless you begin to confront the reality of the situation through studied conversation, conflict will ensue. The needy member will demand more than a group can provide, and members will feel cheated when week after week, their needs get swallowed up by the ECR member's concerns.

For example, in one group, the leader explained privately that no more than fifteen minutes of any meeting could be directly devoted to the ECR person (for prayer, sharing, or updates). During social time before, after, and between meetings, each member would respond as able. The leader also advised the ECR member to join a support group that focused on the particular issue. (Christian counseling, support or recovery groups, or other professional services can provide great backup in situations that move beyond the group's ability to respond adequately.) The member could attend support sessions without having to leave the small group.

The small group can be a loving, caring vehicle working in tandem with more specific and intensive care channels. Other group members are not overlooked, and the ECR person can receive long term care within boundaries that work.

This is definitely a discernment issue for leaders. Again, knowing the kindness-confrontation continuum is very helpful. Such knowledge allows a group to remain compassionate and supportive without draining all its resources to meet one member's needs. A group can give the wonderful gift of community to someone who is in a season of needing care, *if* they respond by walking the small group tightrope in the right way.

Interpersonal Tension

Sometimes people just rub each other the wrong way. Everyone in the group can sense it. It usually doesn't involve overtly sinful behavior. But it can be just as toxic. Underneath may be pride, envy, or simply an inability to connect relationally. One member may not understand another's communication or thinking patterns. Or a member may have annoying behavioral or habitual quirks (like the person who clicks their fingernails or twirls their hair or always has bad breath!) that drive some people nuts. No matter how hard you try, people get on each other's nerves. You can try to dismiss this in the name of kindness, thinking, "People will be people." Or you can do the right thing and confront the situation, name the tension, and seek to improve group dynamics.

Interpersonal tension may develop between a small group leader and a group member. Effective leadership — moving people toward accountability, asking harder questions — may cause tension as people are faced with their habits, fears, and sin.

At Willow Creek, we do everything in teams and in small groups, including many staff groups. When tension developed between two members of a staff group that I (Russ) was leading, I confronted each party individually and said, "I'd just like to ask you a question. What's your deal with so-and-so?" Each responded by saying, "Oh, did you notice that, too?" I said, "Yes. Would you set some time aside for the two of you to get together?" I just got the two of them moving toward each other.

What if I had let the conflict fester instead of asking each individual a simple question? What if I had avoided saying something that might be a little uncomfortable? I can tell you what would have happened — relational breakdown throughout the group and loss of respect for me, the leader!

Instead, I heeded the signal that the situation might get serious and went after it, just in case. And as soon as I said, "What's going on with so-and-so? I just wanted to see what's up," the staff members were embarrassed that the group and I had noticed. It was additional motivation for them to reconcile their differences. And we all avoided the temptation to go to others, rather than to the people who were experiencing the tension.

Teaching Conflict Resolution Skills

We are both closely involved with elders at Willow Creek. (Russ served as an elder for several years, and Bill's wife is currently on the elder board.) Willow elders are responsible for handling conflict that has potential to create division in the body or among staff members. (Most conflicts are handled in the small group structure, but elders handle complex, serious situations.) We've seen people operate in default mode, ignoring biblical patterns and going to everyone but the person involved, using excuses like, "I need prayer for this situation, and I need your advice on how to . . ."

We've seen it over and over again from the vantage point of leading the small groups ministry in different churches. The pattern is too familiar — people ignore Scripture, assuming the Bible doesn't apply when they're hurt or mad. You've probably seen it, too. If they've got an ax to grind with someone, the last thing they want to hear is God's Word on the matter.

And that's why, when conflict arises, you will have to point people to Scripture.[3] If someone is avoiding necessary confrontation in the name of kindness, the conflict resolution process mandated in Matthew can be used to push the person to confront the situation and manage the conflict.

God is deeply concerned with the body's unity and the potential for unhealthy conflict to destroy the body. Matthew 5:23–24 grants us permission to leave a public worship service in order to begin the reconciliation process with an offended brother or sister in Christ. It's the one time when you can walk away—leave whatever you're doing—to go and fix the problem. Jesus was clear: "Therefore, if you are offering your gift at the altar and there remember that your brother has something against you, leave your gift there in front of the altar. First go and be reconciled to your brother; then come and offer your gift."

Notice the containment strategy, keeping conflict between the people involved. The same strategy is presented in Matthew 18:15: "If your brother sins against you, go and show him his fault, just between the two of you." When conflict breaks out, immediately intercept it, and work it out *between the two of you.* Despite your inclination to adopt the kindness-will-fix-this approach, Scripture calls us to confront sin directly to maintain community bonds.

But some people are quick to confront and eager to reconcile, sometimes ignoring the loving spirit in which conflict is to be pursued. Perhaps they're careless with their words or didn't learn in their families how to express kindness during conflict. For them, confrontation comes easily, almost naturally. But it is not always healthy. They need to remember Ephesians 4:15, which emphasizes speaking the truth in *love*. This will tilt them back toward greater kindness and push them to take the edge off their words.

Conflict can be a great source of personal and community growth. Listen to the words of Dr. Jean Vanier, a former naval officer who later chose to create small communities for the mentally disabled. Living and serving among such wonderful people taught him the nature of true community, as well as the need for love, truth, and forgiveness. These seeds produce the fruit of reconciliation.

> Too many people come into community to find something, to belong to a dynamic group, to discover a life which approaches the ideal. If we come into community without knowing the reason we

> come is to learn to forgive and be forgiven seven times seventy-seven times, we will soon be disappointed....
>
> To forgive is also to understand the cry behind the behavior. People are saying something through their anger and/or anti-social behavior. Perhaps they feel rejected. Perhaps they feel that no one is listening to what they have to say or maybe they feel incapable of expressing what is inside them. Perhaps the community is being too rigid or too legalistic and set in its ways; there may even be a lack of love and of truth. To forgive is also to look into oneself and to see where one should change, where one should also ask for forgiveness and make amends.
>
> To forgive is to recognize once again—after separation—the covenant which binds us together with those we do not get along with well; it is to be open and listening to them once again. It is to give them space in our hearts. That is why it is never easy to forgive. We too must change. We must learn to forgive and forgive every day, day after day. We need the power of the Holy Spirit to open up like that.[4]

Indeed we do. And we need the Spirit to help us meet the reconciliation challenge as we walk the tightrope between loving kindness and truthful confrontation. The result is a courageous venture into healthy conflict—conflict that honors God and produces transformation.

Our small groups' protective disposition toward community—protecting it, guarding it, shepherding people through healthy conflict—is of utmost importance. When you understand how God sees community, it takes your breath away, and it makes you want to guard it all the more. This will be a difficult tightrope for you to walk, but we can promise, it is worth it.

When engaging in necessary conflict at Willow Creek, the elders invoke this saying as they enter the fray: "Protect the bride." Whenever the unity of the body is in jeopardy, the gospel may be compromised. Therefore, above all things, we must protect the bride. In our churches, groups, and relationships, this is the standard. Dealing with conflict in healthy ways is vital to the Christian community; the oneness of the bride and the testimony of the gospel hang in the balance. And there is no room for compromise.

Chapter Five

taking it to the streets

MEETING THE IMPACT CHALLENGE BY BALANCING TASK AND PEOPLE

We hear two common refrains when we teach at conferences or consult with church staffs. In often sad or desperate tones, people ask, "How do we get people in our home groups to get out and serve somewhere?" Others say, "We get so caught up with serving, getting the task done, that there's no time for building community. What can we do?" Task versus people — the battle rages in all kinds of groups. But it must be fought and won.

Central to any church's edification process is mobilizing its servants through small groups. The impact challenge addresses the need for groups to balance time with people and the call to serve, to carry out the mission, but not at the expense of members' lives. When this goal is met, the world sees the church in action, which can have a profound impact.

According to a recent poll, 51 percent of respondents believe that religion is losing influence in America.[1] Compare that with a poll taken a year earlier, fresh in the wake of the September 11 terrorist attacks, when 71 percent believed that religious influence was increasing. Since the 1950s, response has ranged from 14 percent of Americans who believed religion was gaining influence to a pre-9/11 high of 48 percent.[2] People likely perceive that religion has influence when religious people (in America, this is primarily those who call themselves Christians) have a positive influence. Our actions—through the church and in the world—are often the only Bible others will read and the only means by which to judge the authenticity of our claims. But how can groups accomplish a task and connect with people in ways that serve the body and impact the world?

Mutually Exclusive Aims?

On one end of the impact continuum, you face the task or ministry. This is especially true in the wide variety of groups and teams focused primarily on accomplishing a particular ministry. At Willow Creek, groups that gather regularly for service range from our elders and board of directors to teams that help in our CARS ministry, in which men and women repair and service autos for single moms and give cars to people in need. (Last year our members donated over 1,000 cars to this ministry; these cars are used for parts or were sold at auctions or repaired, depending on their condition. Over 200 cars were given away to needy families.) Our food pantry feeds the poor, while parking teams and ushers help people navigate onto our campus and into an auditorium seat. Programming and production teams create weekly services and special events. And small groups in our Harvest food-service ministry meet before or after services, to prepare food that people consume at meals, during meetings, and at specialized ministry events. It is clear to us that building community in a task group is hard, especially if the only contact members have is while doing the task.

Serving together is not solely the prerogative of task-focused groups. Small groups that meet in homes, in offices, at church, or in restaurants (for community building, prayer, and Scripture study) encounter the task issue as well. Though they sometimes devote time for service inside or outside Willow Creek, they focus mostly on the other end of the continuum — the people in the group.

The impact continuum, whether you look at it from the vantage point of a serving group or a community group, shapes up like this:

Men's, women's, couples', family, or neighborhood groups — it doesn't matter. If we're in a people-focused group, how can we mobilize members to service? If we lead a task group, how can we get the work done on time and with excellence yet provide a sense of family or community while serving?

One thing is clear: groups cannot afford to focus on one end or the other. Look at how Jesus met the impact challenge in his group: "He appointed twelve — designating them apostles — that they might be with him [a focus on people] and that he might send them out to preach ... [the call to a task]" (Mark 3:14). Community groups miss something if they only meet in homes, do Bible studies, build relationships, and provide basic nurture. Likewise, task teams or serving groups that meet only to get a job done are overlooking the opportunity to enter into one another's lives.

The Task Is the Tool

First, let's look at groups formed to accomplish a task. (But you community group people keep reading; you may find some great ideas here as well!) Task-related groups offer a terrific opportunity to develop people *through* the task, helping them build each other up through works of service. This is Ephesians 4:11–13 in action: "It was he [Jesus] who gave some to be . . . pastors and teachers, to prepare God's people for works of service, so that the body of Christ may be built up until we all reach unity in the faith and in the knowledge of the Son of God and become mature, attaining to the whole measure of the fullness of Christ."

Notice the centrality of serving in the maturation process. *The task is the tool.* In other words, tasks do not distract from the growth process; they actually enhance it! The Bible describes tasks as fundamental to spiritual progress. Sadly, many churches divorce task from growth, thinking that real discipleship takes place only through Bible study or sermons.

When Jesus wanted to challenge his followers, he sent them out on a kingdom mission to test their character and put hands and feet to his teaching (Matt. 10, Luke 10). The task often exposed their weaknesses or petty squabbles. The tensions of getting work done together uncovered character flaws. These tasks gave Jesus teachable moments to pause right in the midst of getting a job done and say, "Wait a minute, we're missing the point of who I am and what I want you to be about." It also gave him the opportunity to affirm the spiritual victories of their two-by-two mission trips: "I saw Satan fall like lightning from heaven" (Luke 10:18).

Isn't it interesting to reflect on parables? The moral of one story devoted to servanthood is an oft-used church phrase: "Well done, good and faithful servant." In other words, those who serve are evaluated as doing well spiritually. Serving provides great opportunities to grow people up, opportunities that are seldom provided by finishing another curriculum series.

Humble service will develop the group's heart and display the leader's character. When Jesus wanted to show ultimate love to his group, he wrapped a towel around his waist and did the most menial of tasks for the members of his little community. Are we as leaders prepared to set the servanthood standard?

One pastor who regularly conducts leadership retreats understands this well. Intentionally arriving early at the retreat center, he would assign menial tasks to his people. "We're here a little early, and some jobs at the retreat center didn't get done. Cindy, could you take care of mopping up the floors? Bob, can you clean the toilets? Mike, can you make sure the kitchen sinks are cleaned up, and Rita, can you help over here?" And then he observed their attitudes, facial expressions, and activities. He used tasks to test the characters they were bringing to the leadership development party. And then, throughout the weekend while they were serving and growing together, he personally modeled what he was teaching.

Problem: The Task Always Wins

Developing people through serving sounds good, doesn't it? But there is a problem: *tasks take time*. You have to identify the work to be done, organize the group, and lead the task to completion.

Building community in the midst of performing a task only makes things more difficult, because task groups and serving teams in most churches don't have the time to put the job aside to focus on people. Groups can't say, "Well, let's just pray together this time and forget handing out food to the poor. I sense God really wants us to speak to him right now." Unacceptable – the task is crying out and has to be done.

But the community opportunity is still there, more than we might think. Why? Because people are already gathering regularly for the sake of the task. It should be easier to build community with those who serve together. People gather throughout the church to get things done, so let's seize these community opportunities.

When we work with other churches, we ask how many small groups they have. Then we map the existing ministry structure, discover places people are gathering to get something done, and point out the opportunity to form a group. Pastors' eyes light up as they begin to see groups where they once saw only teams. Mission boards, Christian education committees, prayer teams, and other gatherings can be moved gradually toward the community end of the continuum, combining task and relationship.

The zillion-dollar question is this: How can you help task people slow down long enough to get to know each other? Here are some ideas.

Your choir meets regularly, so try having them rehearse for approximately thirty minutes or so and then take twenty minutes to break up into small groups to discuss life's issues and needs. A church we worked with does this. They end their group time in prayer, which allows those not connected to groups elsewhere in the church a chance to build some initial relationships. Then they return to choir practice.

People already connected to other groups don't mind the brief but focused time of prayer and relationship building, and the unconnected take initial steps toward community. Once people taste community, new groups will form.

A men's group at Willow Creek meets weekly to complete construction projects. Over a year ago they added a community component to their time together—a few minutes to pray and connect. This fueled a desire for more time together, so they added a monthly meeting in a home, away from the task. Their spouses observed what was happening in the lives of these hard-hat-wearing, hammer-wielding construction guys and asked if they could join. The group now has a monthly gathering that includes the men's families, for dinner, prayer, study, and fellowship.

Willow Creek has become a church of groups, because we've seized opportunities to connect people through tasks. It would be very difficult to get all of our people into traditional home groups, but the serving group option opens the doors to limitless points of gathering, especially for those who are active and enjoy working. And serving groups are great for welcoming seekers who might otherwise feel awkward sitting in a discussion group for a couple hours. If we hadn't learned to connect tasks with community, we'd probably only have two-thirds of our people at Willow Creek connected to little communities.

Whether in a choir or any other serving context, though, the ultimate problem for serving groups is that when task and community building compete, the task always wins. The time allocated for people and task comes into conflict.

When choir rehearsal goes poorly, and it is three weeks before the Easter musical, the task wins. Everyone realizes how valuable moments of community are, but you can't just say, "Oh, well, forget rehearsal. It's time to share life stories." The task can't be done poorly or partially. It's a tension that will never go away. That is why we recommend connections outside of task time, such as short retreats or an occasional overnight with your serving group. These connections will help you focus on the people side of the continuum before you tackle the task again.

Community Feels Sooo Good

The challenge in serving groups is that the task always wins, and the difficulty with community groups is similar: people or relationships always win. That is, it always wins until the group understands how serving together can transform their small community. But it's hard for people to imagine this until they experience it together.

A few years ago, I (Russ) was in a couples' group that included a woman irrepressibly possessed of a mercy gift. You probably know someone like this. Every time they come to a meeting, they tell yet another story of someone they have found to help.

As we approached Christmas, this woman described to us a ministry that provides gifts to orphaned children, and we stumbled onto an idea. What if she could make the connections necessary for our group to touch the lives of a couple of these kids?

Within weeks, we were all gathered in our basement surrounded by what seemed like a mountain of gifts, wrapping paper, and ribbons. As we listened to stories of the two boys who would receive our presents, our hearts began to melt. And soon our hearts were melded together, by finding out how our little community could touch others through our service.

Our group was never the same again. We learned that by moving from the community end of the continuum toward the task end, we ended up enriching our experience of community all over again.

Looking back, I'm not sure why we were so surprised. After all, Jesus told us this is the nature of life in the kingdom. Luke reported Jesus' words about this in Acts 20:35: "It is more blessed to give than to receive." When we extend our exclusive focus on community and give ourselves in service, we experience exponential blessings in deeper relationships.

Several years ago, seasoned church consultant Lyle Schaller analyzed the effectiveness of men's groups he had observed. Among his observations were these two comments that emphasize the need for walking the tightrope:

- The most cohesive groups eat together at least seven or eight times a year. One of the most effective ways to kill a men's group is to eliminate that monthly meal!
- The most cohesive men's groups usually have at least one major project annually that requires people to work with their hands. This normally requires more hands than are readily available in the group. Thus the project serves as an entry point for newcomers, the young, the aged, and more introverted men. It may also offer a unique opportunity to affirm those with nonverbal skills.[3]

Every group has opportunities to build community and serve together. When this tension is managed right, groups begin serving together. The task group must rediscover the community component; community groups must help people recognize that true community is revived in service to others.

The tightrope gets balanced like this:

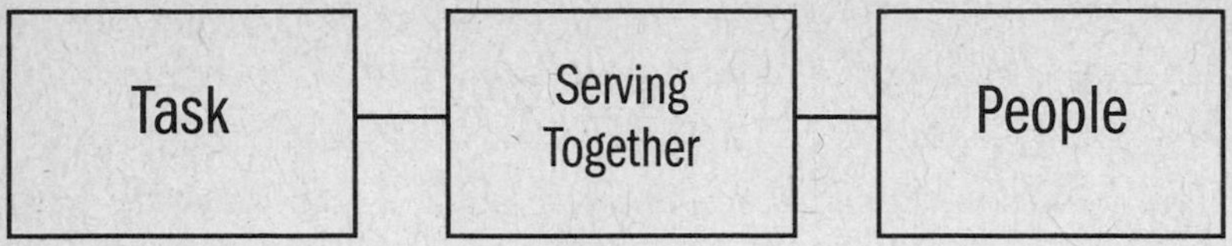

We've seen the benefit of trying to accomplish a task while relating to the people on the team or in the group, or at least to face the reality of this tension, again and again. When groups begin serving together, the result is a high-impact force for increasing the quality of the task and the depth of relationships. That's how churches become filled with increasing numbers of loving communities that serve together and serving communities that love one another.

Bringing Community to the Task

In our experience, serving teams face the most tension when it comes to the impact challenge. Community groups can easily find ways to serve, whether through short-term opportunities within their church, in parachurch organizations, or through connections arranged by group members. The hardest part of adding a serving component to community groups is overcoming the inertia to just hang together.

The challenge for serving groups isn't as simple, which is why the rest of this chapter presents so many ideas for helping task teams build community. Task teams really can become experts at walking the tightrope of serving *together*. After all, these groups are already great at rallying a team to accomplish an objective. Now they can add the objective of building great relationships.

Be Okay at the "101 Level"

In *The Seven Deadly Sins of Small Group Ministry,* we described different levels of intensity at which groups tend to function.[4] The intensity varies according to meeting frequency and length, curriculum choice, format, connections between meetings, and intended outcome. To create some basis for discussing these differences, we adopted language from American higher education, which designates introductory classes as 101-level courses, more rigorous classes as 201- or 301-level courses, and senior-year classes as 401-level courses.

Similarly, we informally designated our groups as 101, 201, 301, or 401 groups to reflect differences in intensity. These are not hard and fast categories, and we don't use these labels outside leadership circles. (No one at the church would say, "I'm in a 301 group.") Here is a comparison of the different levels.

- The 101 groups are entry-level groups focused on connecting members to one another and to the church and on helping people discover basic fellowship and explore introductory spiritual development.
- The 201 groups begin to introduce a regular curriculum or study and encourage members toward a moderate level of openness and accountability. They tend to meet formally at least twice a month.
- The 301 groups could be thought of as disciple-making groups. These groups meet regularly for in-depth Bible study, prayer, and accountability. Their members view learning as increasingly important and see their groups as places of primary care and longer-term relationship. These groups often meet three or four times a month.

- The 401 groups take everything a step further by meeting weekly, connecting between meetings, pursuing intentional development and growth, and exploring leadership roles in the body. "Doing life deeply together" is a phrase we use to describe the community experienced in the 401-level group environment.

Based on this framework, we will talk periodically to our serving small group leaders about the high value they provide when they simply move people toward the people end of the continuum through a 101-level experience. If leaders will simply focus on group connection and basic spiritual orientation, God will bless their efforts.

The goal is not to tack a three-hour Bible study onto a serving obligation. That's not the point. The point is to say, "With the time that we have and with what we do together, how can we leverage all of that to become more like Jesus Christ?"

The answer might be something as simple as encouraging people to use the fifteen minutes before they serve for a time of sharing and prayer. When leaders include prayer and mutual support in their meeting routine, small group members deepen their connections.

The reason for this is stated by Jesus in Matthew 18:20: "For where two or three come together in my name, there am I with them." When we gather for the sake of connecting people with each other and with Christ, he is the first one to show up!

"Be with" along the Way

While developing Willow's small group ministry, we ran into a problem many of you will understand. As we highlighted the importance of small group leaders and transformational meetings, leaders worked hard to make each gathering everything it could be. That was good to a degree, but it produced an unanticipated consequence.

If leaders didn't experience a *Wow!* (you know, the ones that rival the Transfiguration or Pentecost) every time, they wondered what had gone wrong. Serving group leaders, pressed by the urgency of the task, couldn't even begin to compete with groups that experienced a *Wow!* at almost every meeting.

So we coined a new phrase for leaders and small groups: the *be with* factor. It was simply defined as all the time people had to be with each other: Leaders can be with their group members and group members can be with each other. And in serving groups, members could be with each other not only during a 101 sharing and prayer time; they could be with each other at every phase of the task and between meetings.

To "be with" people along the way means catching moments of community with folks, even on the fly. Willow task group leaders do this so well. I (Bill) saw a group leader in Harvest, our food-service ministry, pull aside a team member to say, "Can I make an observation? You give the gift of encouragement when you serve. I watched that man's disposition change just because of how you talked to him and affirmed him when you handed him his plate." When you witness an interaction like that, you see a great example of a leader bringing a relationship-building moment to the task. You can bet that leader and group member have a growing friendship in Christ after an interchange like that.

You don't have to stop, create a circle around a table, and have a bunch of people look at each other in order to have a community experience. While rich and deep relationships can't be founded solely on an on-the-fly rhythm, wonderful things can happen when two people seize moments of community while serving together. Even pausing together to say, "How're you doing—really?" can produce openings to renewed levels of relational growth. As the task permits, members can pause to pray or to share something that can be followed up on at the next meeting.

Encourage serving group members to forego talking about last night's baseball game during their task and instead ask, "Hey, can I follow up on a prayer request with you?" Or as they pass each other while doing the task, "I thought of you in my prayer time. I want to encourage you." It's doing small things in the moment, but the opportunity is there consistently, because people are already coming together.

If you lead a serving group, you can prepare your members for these short but important spiritual moments. Assume your serving group meets fifteen minutes before the task, and everyone goes around the circle to share. You pray together before everyone goes about the task. As the circle ends, you can encourage people to keep sharing as they work. It will create a *be with* dynamic.

If you have a little devotional time just before you go out and serve together, the topic of the devotional can trigger conversation. You can end a brief moment of reflection and prayer by bridging into task time with a suggestion such as, "While we're working together today, let's continue our reflection on this topic by asking each other where we need to take a next step in this area of our growth." Giving permission and a little direction will work wonders.

Some people have the perception that task groups don't make disciples, that discipleship only happens when we gather in a circle to drink coffee and study a book like Romans. But if you try touching people in the right way, even in an on-the-fly moment, you will be amazed at how it will promote another step of growth. Some of

Willow Creek's most profound stories of transformation come from serving groups.

Be Prepared for Special Occasions

Special occasions can be utilized for building into people if we simply plan ahead. These include birthday celebrations, special dinners, retreats, and other events. Regular serving gatherings may be limited to checking in with each other, briefly talking, and sharing prayer needs. Try saying, "We don't have much time around our task. Could we consider getting together outside our normal serving time?" You might be surprised at how responsive people will be.

Serving groups often create an extended gathering time two to four times a year, such as dinner before or after a service, at a time outside the group's scheduled task.

We strongly believe in small group retreats. More community is built in an overnight retreat than we can get in three to six months of small group meetings. So if you're worried about your group's duties tilting too strongly toward tasks, schedule a couple of times to get away. You'll be able to leverage those retreat results through the ensuing months of serving.

Other groups, like the construction team mentioned earlier, add additional meetings to the group rhythm. One group of ushers at Willow Creek has found this to be effective. Ushering at our church involves many tasks around a service (part of what we call Service Ministries). They'll meet briefly each week, but their task sometimes puts great demands on them – someone has a problem, another usher calls in sick or is late, a visitor has a special need or is suddenly ill. As a result, the group's community time gets compromised.

So these ushers gather for dinner once a month, connecting for prayer, deeper fellowship, and mutual need meeting. In addition there are one-on-one gatherings during the week as friendships form in the group. The group also supplements their monthly gatherings with other connections, such as an annual retreat.

Your group can brainstorm together about creating special occasions for enhancing the bonds between members. It only takes one or two things. Sharing holiday traditions, celebrating birthdays, and connecting at kids' sports events may provide opportunities for building relationships. Perhaps using an existing social calendar is the best way to go, since people are going to be somewhere doing something anyway. Whatever it is, such occasions can keep you serving together.

Be Available to Help with the Next Step

Small groups, whether serving or otherwise, can be plagued by an old notion. It is a by-product of the enormous contribution from those devoted to discipleship, which we mentioned in our discussion on the development challenge.

Because small groups are supposed to help people grow spiritually, some leaders wrongly conclude it is their job to be sure their little community takes every member from pagan to missionary in twelve months. Sounds like a group on spiritual steroids! It implies that spiritual growth happens quickly, when in reality it takes a lifetime. But most small group leaders we talk to have a vague sense that anything short of that is failure. Passive group members may join a group for discipleship and then feel disappointed at their slow progress.

Here is a dose of reality: No small group can bear the entire spiritual growth responsibilities designed for the whole body of Christ to carry. We didn't grow to our current stage of spiritual maturity (or immaturity, some of our closest friends might suggest) that way, and neither did you. At best, we were in our groups for an average run of two to four years, and the combination of many communities and people contributed to who we have become over a long time. That is why a variety of groups and experiences are essential. No, not group hopping, and we are not advocating tossing out enduring relationships like used cars. But realize that although friendships can last a lifetime, it is often the new relationships in your life that challenge you to grow. People with fresh ideas, different gifts, or different ethnic backgrounds from those in your group or neighborhood may bring you to a new spiritual edge. So you don't have to do it all in one group.

In most groups, you can promote spiritual growth simply by assessing where members are at in their spiritual progress and helping them take their next step. You don't know how long you'll be together. People move, get transferred, retire to Florida, or die. You may be together for a year, or you may have ten years. But usually all you can do is say, "Where are you today? How can we help get you to the next place God wants you?"

That's why the focus on something like the shepherding plan in chapter 2 matters so much. For example, not long ago I (Russ) was working with a guy in my small group, trying to discern the next step Christ was calling him to take. The five Gs gave me a framework for assessing his progress as a whole, not just one aspect. Though I didn't have the chart on the table in front of us, I had each of the five Gs in mind as our conversation flowed from topic to topic.

While thinking through the Gifts G, I asked questions about where this man was serving. Looking back, I think the Holy Spirit prompted me to focus on this. As I probed carefully into what he had learned in the various areas in which he had already served, he hit the punch line: "You know," he said, "I really don't know what my spiritual gifts are."

If I hadn't been using our shepherding plan framework, I don't know if I would have mentioned spiritual gifts, because it's not a regular topic for discussion in our group. But by using a plan that emphasized next steps in a few key areas, I played a role in helping him discover a spiritual gift of teaching. He's now taking his first steps at getting involved with a ministry in which his gift will be used.

I don't know what other next steps of growth will come about through our relationship. I suspect that, as with most people God has connected me to, my influence may have a limited duration. But if all I accomplish with him is this one next step, I'm glad. It's opened up a whole new area of his life for him.

If every person in a serving group can think in terms of each person's next step rather than trying to handle everything in their spiritual growth, remarkable development can happen. When you serve alongside others, God will make it clear why he has brought you into a person's life as an aid to their next step.

No leader and no group should feel burdened to take people through the whole range of their growth. This is about saying, "Where are you today? And how, in the midst of this task and what we're trying to do together, can we take you to the next step?"

Be Focused on the Goal

Look at any sports team or work group in the marketplace and you will see that rallying around a worthy goal helps people develop a special kind of community. For example, one sports championship brings teams back for repeated reunions. Achieving a major objective paves the way for many subsequent reflections on cherished memories. Veteran military units stay in touch until the last man standing falls. Focusing on accomplishing a goal can produce a deep sense of connection.

Accomplishing a goal is a good thing. Serve well. It's not acceptable to do a poor job at a task in the name of fellowship. There's no place for saying, "It is more important to pray and study; the task will get done when we have time." You can't do that. Excellent service performed with an open heart makes a difference. People's real needs must be met, and that won't happen by simply limiting our group efforts to studying and praying together. And meeting people's needs will enhance the opportunity to form growing, authentic relationships.

There are plenty of serving opportunities in every church. Each opportunity can help community groups serve or help task teams find ways to connect people and build them up. If you tend to focus on people and relationships, remember that serving together will stretch your group spiritually and relationally. Focusing on a goal the group can accomplish together will build even deeper community.

Stay focused on the goal. Serve well — together. You have to do the task anyway, so do the together part well, too.

Be Prayerful

Have you noticed one constant in almost everything we've said about building relational depth? Prayer. Prayer is a great way to build relationships because it is a context in which people will open up, be more vulnerable, follow up with each other, and witness God's work through his answers.

You can pray along the way, between meetings, over the phone. There are many ways that groups who are task-heavy can include prayer. It's easier to pray or share prayer requests when members serve next to each other. It doesn't work for parking team members to yell across the lot, "Hey, how's your mom?" But you can get everyone together, even as a parking crew, and sit around a table for a few minutes of prayer after you've finished your duties.

In fact, you can be sure of one thing. If you use prayer as your default mechanism whenever you want to build up community, you will advance your serving group's spiritual and relational experience. When in doubt, pray.

The Payoff – One Life at a Time

A senior pastor from Michigan asked me (Bill) for guidance on his church's emerging small groups ministry. He brought the new small groups pastor with him, which was impressive because the church had only 350 members. I wondered how they got focused so quickly on small groups, making it such a high staffing priority. Over lunch, the pastor introduced me to Brad, asking Brad to tell his story – one he would later bravely tell at our annual Willow Creek Small Groups Conference, to an audience of 3,400!

Four years earlier Brad and his wife had been living the good life, with a few excursions into the world of recreational drug use. A veterinarian by profession, Brad made a lot of money, owned a big house, drove expensive cars, and partied often. Life was fast and exciting; everything was going great.

Except for one small problem. He was slowly sinking into a pattern of addiction, which eventually started to ruin his otherwise picture-perfect marriage. His emotional life was unraveling. In a fit of desperation, his wife turned to the church, ultimately finding Christ.

Partly in an effort to save her from what he suspected was a cult, Brad showed up at church. Actually, he finally admitted that she had dragged him there. But he had been determined to show her she was deceived, caught up in a religious sideshow that had no basis in fact or reality.

Each week Brad was warmly greeted by ushers and sat patiently through services, looking for his opportunity to expose the charade. You can imagine his surprise when, sometime around his fifth week, a hospitality team greeter asked, "Hey, would you like to serve with us? We need some help handing out the weekly programs."

Politely but directly Brad said, "Can I tell you something? First of all, I don't even believe in God. And second, I don't even think I like this church." The greeter responded, "That's okay. Can you do this?" and stretched out his arm to hand Brad a program. "Can you hand these out each week? That's no big deal, is it?" Brad conceded. But then the other shoe dropped. There was a catch.

"Before we hand out programs, we meet together for prayer — it's part of what we do. Since you have agreed to help, you'll need to be there about twenty minutes early for the prayer time." It was too late to back out, so Brad said, "I'll tell you what. I'll show up early, but I'm not saying a word."

Brad looked me in the eye at lunch and filled in the blanks of the story. "Week after week I showed up and listened to these men pray, share their hearts, and meet each other's needs. I thought to myself, *They really believe this stuff!* For three months I had an open window into their lives — the good, the bad, and the ugly." After experiencing the team atmosphere and seeing lives change, Brad felt God at work in him.

One hospitality team member also led a seeker group, designed to address the questions many skeptics ask about Christ and Christianity. He invited Brad to attend — three times. After two negative responses, Brad finally said yes and joined a little community of skeptics just like him. A few months later, he became a follower of Christ. And over the next few years, Brad matured in group life and eventually became a small group leader and coach.

The journey from skeptic to leader took almost four years, and now Brad was beginning a new adventure. Just months before our lunch, the pastor had rocked Brad's world again, by asking him to lead the growing small groups ministry at the church. And Brad accepted, cutting his veterinary work back so he could come on staff part time. So here they were — a pastor and his new part-time small groups pastor, asking how to grow the ministry that had changed their lives so dramatically. It was a lunch I will never forget.

And it all happened because one task group leader *really got it* and said, "What if we reach out in the midst of the task and change lives? What if we provide a connection to community in the midst of the task? Maybe — just maybe — we can touch the life of someone far from God."

Never downplay the opportunity you have to foster spiritual growth through works of service. It could be the spiritual-growth experience of your life!

Chapter Six

guess who's coming to small group!

MEETING THE CONNECTION CHALLENGE BY BALANCING OPENNESS AND INTIMACY

In *The Kingdom of God Is a Party,* Tony Campolo describes an event that took place when he was in Hawaii for a speaking engagement. Because of the time change — Tony lives on the East Coast — he kept waking up around 2:30 in the morning and going to a coffee shop for donuts. This is what he writes:

> Up a side street I found a little place that was still open. I went in, took a seat on one of the stools at the counter, and waited to be served. This was one of those sleazy places that deserves the name, "greasy spoon." I mean I did not even touch the menu. I was afraid that if I opened the thing something gruesome would crawl out. But it was the only place I could find.
>
> The fat guy behind the counter came over and asked me, "What d'ya want?"

I told him. I said I wanted a cup of coffee and a donut.

He poured a cup of coffee, wiped his grimy hand on his smudged apron, and then he grabbed a donut off the shelf behind him. I'm a realist. I know that in the back room of that restaurant, donuts are probably dropped on the floor and kicked around. But when everything is out front where I could see it, I really would have appreciated it if he had used a pair of tongs and placed the donut on some wax paper.

As I sat there munching on my donut and sipping my coffee at 3:30 in the morning the door of the diner suddenly swung open and, to my discomfort, in marched eight or nine provocative and boisterous prostitutes.

It was a small place and they sat on either side of me. Their talk was loud and crude. I felt completely out of place and was just about to make my getaway when I overheard the woman beside me say, "Tomorrow's my birthday. I'm going to be thirty-nine."

Her "friend" responded in a nasty tone, "So what do you want from me? A birthday party? What do you want? Ya want me to get you a cake and sing 'Happy Birthday'?"

"Come on," said the woman sitting next to me. "Why do you have to be so mean? I was just telling you, that's all. Why do you have to put me down? I was just telling you it was my birthday. I don't want anything from you. I mean, why should you give me a birthday party? I've never had a birthday party in my whole life. Why should I have one now?"

When I heard that, I made a decision. I sat and waited until the women had left. Then I called over the fat guy behind the counter and I asked him, "Do they come in here every night?"

"Yeah!" he answered.

"The one right next to me, does she come here every night?"

"Yeah!" he said. "That's Agnes. Yeah, she comes in here every night. Why d'ya wanta know?"

"Because I heard her say that tomorrow is her birthday," I told him. "What do you say you and I do something about that? What do you think about us throwing a birthday party for her—right here—tomorrow night?"

A cute smile slowly crossed his chubby cheeks and he answered with measured delight, "That's great! I like it! That's a great idea!" Calling to his wife, who did the cooking in the back room, he shouted, "Hey! Come out here! This guy's got a great idea. Tomorrow's Agnes's birthday. This guy wants us to go in with him and throw a birthday party for her—right here—tomorrow night!"

His wife came out of the back room all bright and smiley. She said, "That's wonderful! You know Agnes is one of those people who is really nice and kind, and nobody does anything nice and kind for her."

"Look," I told them, "if it's O.K. with you, I'll get back here tomorrow morning about 2:30 and decorate the place. I'll even get a birthday cake!"

"No way," said Harry (that was his name). "The birthday cake's my thing, I'll make the cake."

At 2:30 the next morning, I was back at the diner. I had picked up some crepe-paper decorations at the store and had made a sign out of big pieces of cardboard that read, "Happy Birthday, Agnes!" I decorated the diner from one end to the other. I had that diner looking good.

The woman who did the cooking must have gotten the word out on the street, because by 3:15 every prostitute in Honolulu was in the place. It was wall-to-wall prostitutes . . . and me!

At 3:30 on the dot, the door of the diner swung open and in came Agnes and her friend. I had everybody ready (after all, I was kind of the M.C. of the affair) and when they came in we all screamed, "Happy birthday!"

Never have I seen a person so flabbergasted . . . so stunned . . . so shaken. Her mouth fell open. Her legs seemed to buckle a bit. Her friend grabbed her arm to steady her. As she was led to sit on one of the stools along the counter we all sang "Happy Birthday" to her. As we came to the end of our singing with "happy birthday dear Agnes, happy birthday to you," her eyes moistened. Then, when the birthday cake with all the candles on it was carried out, she lost it and just openly cried.

Harry gruffly mumbled, "Blow out the candles, Agnes! Come on! Blow out the candles! If you don't blow out the candles, I'm gonna hafta blow out the candles." And, after an endless few seconds, he did. Then he handed her a knife and told her, "Cut the cake, Agnes. Yo, Agnes, we all want some cake."

Agnes looked down at the cake. Then without taking her eyes off it, she slowly and softly said, "Look, Harry, is it all right with you if I . . . I mean is it O.K. if I kind of . . . what I want to ask you is . . . is it O.K. if I keep the cake a little while? I mean, is it all right if we don't eat it right away?"

Harry shrugged and answered, "Sure! It's O.K. If you want to keep the cake, keep the cake. Take it home, if you want to."

"Can I?" she asked. Then, looking at me she said, "I live just down the street a couple of doors. I want to take the cake home, O.K.? I'll be right back. Honest!"

She got off the stool, picked up the cake, and, carrying it like it was the Holy Grail, walked slowly toward the door. As we all just stood there motionless, she left.

When the door closed there was a stunned silence in the place. Not knowing what else to do, I broke the silence by saying, "What do you say we pray?"

Looking back on it now it seems more than strange for a sociologist to be leading a prayer meeting with a bunch of prostitutes in a diner in Honolulu at 3:30 in the morning. But then it just felt like the right thing to do. I prayed for Agnes. I prayed for her salvation. I prayed that her life would be changed and that God would be good to her.

When I finished, Harry leaned over the counter and with a trace of hostility in his voice, he said, "Hey! You never told me you were a preacher. What kind of church do you belong to?"

In one of those moments when just the right words came, I answered, "I belong to a church that throws birthday parties for whores at 3:30 in the morning."

Harry waited a moment and then almost sneered as he answered, "No you don't. There's no church like that. If there was, I'd join it. I'd join a church like that!"

Wouldn't we all? Wouldn't we all like to join a church that throws birthday parties for whores at 3:30 in the morning?

Well, that's the kind of church that Jesus came to create![1]

Christ's Kingdom Is for Everyone

Campolo's story highlights the incredible truth that the kingdom door swings open for all kinds of people. Jesus modeled this kingdom openness for us by inviting tax collectors and sinners, rich and poor, follower and Pharisee, to the table of community. This is the way the church ought to be. And it is how most groups ought to function. But most groups are in the intimacy business, not the openness game. Most groups are eager to find a few folks they connect with and then build deep relationships with them for the rest of their lives. Unfortunately, when groups are closed, it limits the number of connection points for people seeking community life in the local church. After all, that is where many will connect — if groups are open.

When Openness and Intimacy Collide

Suggesting "open groups" is where tension begins, because the need for openness assumes the existence of one end of the continuum — a willingness to welcome new members into the group. If groups don't maintain some sense of availability to those who are unconnected, a church must keep creating new groups to give new folks a place in community. But few churches have enough incoming leaders or the ability to rapidly develop enough new leaders to keep creating groups.

Meanwhile, many churches have committed to developing emerging leaders through an apprentice strategy.[2] They bank on the eventual multiplication of groups that are growing via the ongoing addition of new members to existing little communities, then developing leaders in those growing groups. Connection, leadership development, and continual community growth all demand openness.

At the other end of the continuum is intimacy. Deep, lasting, meaningful relationships require time and intent. Spiritual transformation and relational intimacy both require time. Groups require safety to pursue conflict resolution and create true community. It is the accumulation of experiences together — praying, talking, and serving *together* — that provides the foundation for healthy small group ministry.

When openness and intimacy collide, intimacy usually wins. People will search far and wide for vibrant relational connections and, when they find them, will guard them like a federal prison. Who can blame them? In a transient society filled with vocational nomads, people long for deep connections. They'll put up walls around their community rather than keep that community open and risk losing what they've worked so hard to find.

Groups often disagree about how open they should be, sometimes because of previous relational breakdowns or a bad group experience. The tension groups experience in the connection challenge looks like this:

The Inside-Out Community

God has always created an open chair at the table of community. That's just how he is. Look at his interaction with Abraham and the nation of Israel. He chose them for a redemptive purpose, that one day all nations would be represented in the kingdom community. Whenever God's people sinned and disrupted that plan, God felt frustrated both because they had rebelled and because their rebellion ruined the attractiveness of the community God was creating. Psalm 67 describes Israel as a light intended to draw all nations to the one true God.

That didn't change when Christ invited people to become part of the new community. "I will build My church," he said, "and the gates of Hades will not overpower it" (Matt. 16:18 NASB). Christ called his followers to this intense mission, urging them to travel the globe and preach the gospel everywhere. Christ pushed his followers to both intimacy and openness. As we have already discussed, he prayed that the oneness of his followers would equal that of the Trinity — where connecting with human and divine community portray intimacy at its best!

Yet Christ predicated his prayer for our oneness on an even larger idea, "that the world may believe that you have sent me" (John 17:21, 23). As new Christians in the 1970s, we often sang the refrain, "And they'll know we are Christians by our love," a paraphrase of John 13:35. Yes, they'll have a front-row seat to the awesome life-giving power of God's love by watching Christians love each other. (That's scary!) Our oneness in love is a testimony to God's love and will draw to Christ many who hunger for that kind of love.

But Christ's purposes demand that this intimate community have a cause, a mission beyond itself. This combination of intimacy and openness allows people to experience God's design for people in the body—inclusive community.

To get the idea of inclusive community across to our small group leaders one year, we chose the title "Inside Out" for our annual retreat.

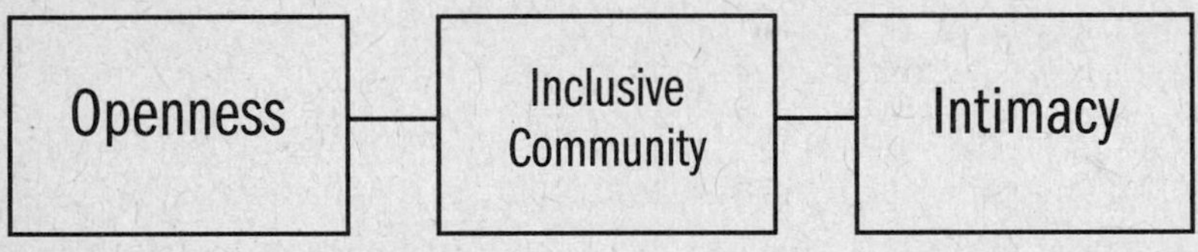

We devoted multiple leadership gatherings to helping people understand how God works in our little communities to accomplish his redemptive purposes. He always has a redemptive purpose in mind; it's in his character.

But those purposes are never intended simply for those on the inside. God is always searching for those who are on the outside looking in. He leaves the flock of ninety-nine to search for the one lost sheep. Like a poor widow seeking a lost coin, he scours the earth seeking what has been lost—his greatest treasure, people. He is the loving father of Luke 15, desperately searching for his rebellious sons and daughters, prodigals who wonder if they will be welcomed home. The answer is always a resounding *Yes!*

And he expects us — now redeemed insiders — to be on the lookout for strays searching for home. To move from the inside out. This is a matter of the heart, as Vanier aptly describes: "A loving community is attractive. And a community which is attractive is by definition welcoming. Life brings new life.... Love can never be static. A human heart is either progressing or regressing. If it is not becoming more open, it is closing and withering spiritually. A community which refuses to welcome — whether through fear, weariness, insecurity, a desire to cling to comfort, or just because it is fed up with visitors — is dying spiritually."[3]

But how does this work? How do you handle the tension of intimacy and openness? Every group has to handle this hot potato. Members ask, "Do we build intimacy, or are we here to add more people and grow the group? After all, if our focus is growth, we cannot build depth. If our focus is relational depth, how can we do that if we keep adding people?"

When a group realizes that openness and intimacy are not mutually exclusive, it can achieve God's purpose for any gathering in Christ — inclusive community. We must pursue the Great Commandment and the Great Commission together, learning how to reach new people while building intimacy in groups. If we don't, God's divine purpose for his people and for our groups will never be realized.

Taking Relational Risks

Sometimes the root of this difficulty is a misunderstanding. Openness results from people coming to a place where they really love each other, which then gets combined with a sense of gratitude for what they've experienced.

First, they find true community and experience love. Correspondingly, they feel grateful to have found a community that meets their needs. The combination of these two experiences, love plus gratitude, puts them at a crossroads. When love and gratitude come together, the question is whether they are now willing to take a risk and extend these experiences to others.

When things work right, people become willing to risk their sense of community. They see someone on the outside looking in and remember how it felt to live without this gift of community. Gratitude for experiencing abundant love makes them willing to share that gift with others. But extending this gift of love for which they are grateful creates vulnerability.

Group members have to be willing to let someone else inside the circle. Any new person alters the group's chemistry. Nobody knows how group dynamics will change once someone new comes in. It could be bad news to the previously loving collection of people. Community is fragile enough that messing with it can be risky.

In fact, openness produces an equation that looks something like this:

Love + Gratitude + *Risk* = **Openness**

Risk aversion arises, however, when a group realizes what is at stake — their hard fought intimacy. Why take such a risk? Why not completely avoid risk, keep their community safe, and let someone else connect the unconnected?

Such thinking is based on a false assumption — that only openness has inherent risks, that no risk is involved in building intimacy.

Intimacy requires enormous risk; just look at a marriage, a business partnership, or a close-knit team. Without risk, there is no community. Building community is dangerous, because it calls us to participate in vulnerability and trust. Listen to Jean Vanier once again:

> Community life is the place where our limitations, our fears and our egoism are revealed to us. We discover our poverty and our weaknesses, our inability to get along with some people, our mental and emotional blocks, our affective or sexual disturbances, our seemingly insatiable desires, our frustrations and jealousies, our hatred and our wish to destroy. While we are alone, we could believe we loved everyone. Now that we are with others, living with them all the time, we realize how incapable we are of loving, how much we deny to others, how closed in on ourselves we are.... Community is the place where the power of the ego is revealed and where it is called to die so that people become one body and give much life.[4]

That last sentence should terrify you. Not so that you become afraid of community, but rather because you understand the incredible rewards that lie ahead for those willing to do the work of building intimacy, taking relational risks involving self-disclosure, confession, and love.

Intimacy begins to develop in a group when two things are present: duration (how long the group has been together) and confidentiality. Time together allows trust to form, and confidentiality ensures it will be kept. When people remain together long enough to feel safe, guess what? They confide their secrets, fears, longings, and hopes. The ever-expanding reservoir of insider information creates an accumulating sense of intimacy, but it has its risks as well. What if someone betrays a confidence? What if, after you share secrets or fears, someone leaves the group? You have ventured out on a relational limb. How fragile is the branch?

Intimacy comes from a combination of duration and confidentiality, plus one other thing: risk. You have to take a risk to tell your secrets. You can have duration and confidentiality, but if you avoid the potentially perilous step of sharing the deeper parts of yourself, you won't achieve much intimacy.

Intimacy is rooted in vulnerability, so it is never hazard free. This little danger transforms the equation to:

Duration + Confidentiality + *Risk* = Intimacy

When we ask small groups to consider adding a new member, people often say, "That's a risky thing to do." And we readily acknowledge that. But don't get fooled into thinking that intimacy is a risk-free deal.

Both intimacy and openness require risk. We could probably make a case that pursuing openness as a group requires *less* risk than being truly intimate with one another. It's much riskier for people to start telling their secrets and bank on the confidentiality of the group. Truth be told, most people will find that someone in their group has a slip of the tongue every now and then, and it heightens the sense of the risk required to find authentic intimacy.

Neither end of the continuum is safe. But to achieve God's purpose of connecting people into an inclusive redemptive community, risk is required at both ends. Christ asks us to balance the risks of openness and intimacy so we keep the tension in the tightrope.

Avoiding the Closed Group Syndrome

Five dynamics keep groups from extending the hand of community to outsiders. Awareness of these tendencies and characteristics will help you work against the natural drift toward closed community.

The Dynamic of Hoarding

We naturally tend to build walls around community to protect it. At Willow Creek, we call this "stockpiling" community. Conventional thinking says that once we have found a great thing, we should keep it to ourselves.

In our first years at Willow, my wife and I (Bill) had an incredible time leading a couples' group that produced lasting change in many of us. Relationships in that group still remain strong, long after the group has ended. Early on, however, we had to navigate choppy waters. When Gail and I discussed birthing a new group someday, a member approached me after the meeting to set me straight. "I'm not feeling very comfortable with that. I don't like the birthing thing; I don't want to destroy the group. It took us over a year to find a small group, and now we have finally found a few friends we like. Don't mess it up."

I was thinking, *At least I know how you really feel!* Her words were ringing in my ears, but one phrase caught my attention. *It took us over a year . . .* I gently challenged her. "Why did it take you so long?"

"There were no groups in the area," she said, "until you started one."

"How did you get into this one?" I asked.

Somewhat perturbed by the question, she responded, "You invited us."

I closed the sale. "You mean we had room for you, so we invited you to the group, and that's how you got here?"

Suddenly the logic hit home to this sharp Ph.D. and she understood. "I get it now," she said, and walked away.

How could someone who took a year to find community suddenly hold it so tightly? Because we are afraid! Because we lose sight of

God's desire to build an increasingly inclusive community. It is our nature to gravitate toward exclusivity in relationships.

But this tendency isn't always the result of harboring a latent attitude of exclusivity; sometimes it stems from busyness. It's not that groups hate newcomers; most group members just don't have the time to build relationships with people outside the group. One group at the church said, "It took us so long to finally get this, we hate to see it break up or add people." We dug further into those and similar comments. Here's what they were really saying: "We're so busy, life's so chaotic—we finally found a place of stability. Please don't mess with it." Unstable work lives, family turmoil, and other sources of constant change had overwhelmed them. Life was so crazy for them that the small group provided the only time during the whole week when they felt consistently cared for.

You can help people wavering between the fear of risk and the sin of selfishness to focus on God's redemptive purposes. When people internalize his purpose to build a redemptive community of surpassing love and gratitude, they can't help sharing it with others who need what the members have experienced. When you take steps to protect confidentiality and allow time for people to rebuild intimacy, you can move people into a balanced rhythm of intimacy and openness.

The Dynamic of Stagnation

Every group drifts toward becoming ingrown. Yet when groups aren't open to new life, they stagnate. They miss what new members offer—fresh vision, other spiritual gifts, innovative perspectives, and new talents and abilities.

It's rare that a group of six to ten people will stay together for more than a couple of years without turning inward and losing its transformational edge. Sometimes a group of dynamic leaders who are involved in strategic and challenging ministry can pull it off. Even then, however, groupthink can set in, making the relationships routine and stale. There are rare exceptions, but the truth is that most closed groups tend to get self-centered. In fact, the durability of a group containing the same people for many years may be the best evidence that they have missed God's intent for Christian community.

I (Bill) cannot imagine our group today without the three guys we've added in the last eighteen months. But there was a time when we looked around the circle and everybody said, "This feels really good right now. We've finally arrived. We're really experiencing the kind of intimacy we have longed for in a men's group." As the conversation continued, we realized we were experiencing a combination of fear, lost vision, and — we had to admit it — selfishness. But each of us also had enough experience at small groups to know how quickly the wonder of intimacy can stagnate. We decided to put our community on the line, adding two men at one point and a third man three months later.

Amazingly, as we look at the group today, the increased openness has created deeper intimacy among us. The unique personalities, stories, gifts, and questions of the new men took us to places we couldn't have gone by ourselves.

My (Russ) habit as Willow Creek's director of small groups was to quiz people on whether their group was open. An interesting pattern emerged. Whenever I met someone who objected to the idea of opening up their group to newcomers, I would ask them why. As expected, they described it as a risky proposition.

Then I would inquire about the last time they had welcomed a newcomer into the group. To a person, they couldn't think of one time they had done this. Ever. I know it's hard to believe, but in scores of conversations over seven years, I never found anyone with an objection to openness who had personally had a bad experience with group openness.

Similarly, among those who were in groups that had added seekers or unconnected believers, no one ever reported a bad experience. Ever. Once again, after scores of conversations, I never found anyone who had actually experienced what closed groups fear — the breakdown of intimacy when a newcomer enters the group. Sure, there are weird people and occasionally some can even be toxic and destroy a community. (But even Bill has had only one such experience in twenty years of group life, so we'd say the risks are very low.)

Maybe I simply talked to the wrong people. That's possible. I suspect there are people who had a negative experience after opening their group. I just never met any of them. No openness bogeyman exists, except in people's minds. Eventually, we built a biblical foundation for God's pattern of inclusiveness, explaining that he is always building a community to reach a community. As we gathered and told more stories about God enriching people and their little communities, we were able to dispel mistaken assumptions about the risks of opening groups to newcomers.

The Dynamic of Mobility

Let's face it. People in our culture often shift geographic locations. The norm is every three to five years. It's not a good thing; but it is a reality, one that will take time to change. Each group we've been in over the years has encountered interruptions in group participation because of employment transfer, family crises, and so on. In retrospect, God was behind most of these moves, redeploying his servants throughout the kingdom. But it did change the group dynamic.

My (Bill) group faced this dynamic after September 11, 2001, when many people lost their jobs. During a season of unemployment, two guys from our men's group were like displaced refugees as they adjusted their schedules for interviews and traveling. Both men tried to stay at the church they loved (Willow) and in the communities where they lived. But apparently God had other plans. As the money ran out and job opportunities arose, both men were required to move. When we finally had to say our farewells, the reality of mobility stared us squarely in the face.

Add to such changes what we at Willow Creek call internal mobility. A new ministry launches, and someone who's been in your group for two or three years tells you they have found their true passion. And off they go to that ministry. Internal mobility happens in any church that is growing, and helping people to discover their spiritual gifts and become all Christ intends. Again, it's not bad, just true.

Our new regional ministry efforts are producing fresh doses of the dynamic of mobility. Now that we are creating new congregations — by the time this book is published, there will be three regional sites in addition to our home campus in South Barrington — mobility is affecting whole segments of our congregation. And since we are a church of small groups, each movement affects group life. Regionalization will ultimately enhance our efforts as groups form in neighborhoods near a Willow campus. But there will always be some mobility because people connect at different places in different eras of their spiritual growth and changes in how they serve all through their Christian lives. Seeker and new believer groups are especially likely to encounter this dynamic.

But our church is convinced that regionalization is one of the surest exhibitions of God's divine purpose for Willow Creek. Perhaps God has been building a community on our main campus for twenty-some years so that ultimately we would be positioned to reach ever-increasing parts of metro Chicago. Ignoring the dynamic of mobility would interrupt planning for Willow's direction and place us at odds with God's vision for building an inclusive community.

Take advantage of the inevitable. People move. Groups cannot ignore this fact. It will definitely impact your group at some point. Once you accept mobility as part of normal group experience, you anticipate it and open your group to those who have been affected by it. People who need a home will certainly come your way.

The Dynamic of Natural Relationship

When we talk about openness, a few folks will say, "I get the deal. You're just trying to get more people into Willow Creek small groups. You're just doing your jobs." To some extent, they are absolutely right. We have a stake in the openness of our groups. If closed groups don't make room, our small group strategy suffers.

Unfortunately, our urgency to connect people to community (for good reasons) sent the message that we were simply meeting some preset agenda. People felt like *we* wanted *them* to stay open so *we* could send *our* people to *their* groups. Groups felt used, and we lost the moral high ground of calling them to Christ's dream of community.

Of course, the people who know us recognized our greater motivation and desire to help people find a pathway to the oneness Jesus prayed they would find. But we needed to communicate more carefully, using words that matched our wishes.

We returned to relational—instead of organizational—language. We modeled and taught how members could be added to groups through natural relational networks at work, in the neighborhood, and in the family. In the ordinary course of relational rhythms, people have opportunities to introduce their friends to other members of the small group. After people connect at services, social events, and other routine activities, friendships develop.

As these friendships grow naturally, inroads into group life become equally natural. After several group members have been introduced to the new folks in the course of normal life, an invitation to a group social event or a regular meeting can ensue. It isn't much different than inviting someone to dinner at your home.

Most of the time, if natural relational rhythms are followed, adding a new member to your group will be a wonderful adventure. Many new relationships will form. Add lots of prayer, communication between group members, enough time, and sensitive interaction with those looking to join the group, and God will make his divine purposes clear, group by group, life by life.

Once you add someone to your group, take time to foster intimacy through redeveloping your covenant.[5] Refreshing your covenant will remind everyone of group values, so each member is clear on what you believe about your community. You can also orient everyone on your intent to reach out and invite people into your group. Putting expectations on the table, including a covenant of confidentiality, will accelerate the rebuilding of intimacy in your group.

As I (Bill) mentioned earlier, my group is revisiting and reforming our covenant. Our four main community values are to create safety, practice authenticity in relationships, engage with truth, and commit to prayer. These are foundational to who we are as a group. We have arrived at these focal points by talking for a few weeks, clearly defining each value, and relating it to each member's expectations and intentions. The process has deepened intimacy. We know what we're about.

We have just added three new people, so it will be a few months before we probably add new members again. But adding people is part of our group's long-term vision. That has never changed. We are always building relationships and remaining open to new people God brings our way. We honor the dynamic of natural relationship. We don't force it but instead trust it will arise naturally through prayer and time.

The Dynamic of Legacy

What's your legacy? What will you leave behind? Will you hoard what God has given or give it away so others' lives can change? What impact will you have on the next generation?

Our purpose in life—given to us by God in Christ—is to enjoy community and extend to others an invitation to participate in the drama of redemption. We leave in our wake the lives we have touched—or ignored, whatever the case may be. By developing apprentice leaders and empowering others to extend the gift of relationship in Christ, we leave a legacy of community that reaches far beyond our immediate circle of influence.

Paul understood this reality. Just read Romans 16 and count the lives he marked—people who, in turn, marked him for eternity. Friends, family, and fellow workers helped him extend community. He refers to several people as "dear friend" and to another as one "whom I love in the Lord" (v. 8). Many who Paul mentioned were "fellow workers" who never let intimacy get in the way of opening the doors of community to all who chose to enter. They built the church and, in the process, came to love each other deeply.

I (Russ) taught small group values to our Willow Creek membership class each month for many years. I ended almost every talk by discussing legacy. I wanted to remind people that they can take only one thing from this world into the next—people. You leave them behind when you die; but one day, because you extended a hand, they will join you.

The next addition to your small group might be the leader who grows up and does things you can't even imagine in ministry. Consider how many lives may be changed by adding just one person to your group.

A Mission Worth Living For

The Texas Army National Guard has a group of special workers called riggers. Their job is to fold and pack the parachutes that soldiers use when jumping from an airplane at 5,000 feet. These people are intensely dedicated to their task. The Rigger's Creed states, "I will be sure—always!" They know that jumpers need assurance that everything regarding their chutes is perfect. Thirty folds are required in the twenty minutes it takes to meticulously pack an MC1-1 military parachute. A jumper has nothing to do with the chute until they put it on before a jump. Trust in the error-free performance of the riggers is all a jumper has to rely on.

The Rigger's Creed further states: "I will never let the idea that a piece of work is 'good enough' make me a potential murderer through a careless mistake or oversight, for I know there can be no compromise with perfection."[6] Riggers know that the parachute business is a life-or-death enterprise. Mistakes cost lives. There is no room for complacency.

Do we approach our kingdom responsibilities with equal fervor? Do we realize that connecting people to community is a life-or-death enterprise? Are we willing to sacrifice our comfort and safety so that others can join us in the grand adventure of kingdom building? It will involve risks, but the mission is worth it. Let's not let the idea that our level of openness is "good enough" make us complacent, turning away countless people who need to find Christ and grow in relationship with him and his people. Let's make the ask, take the risk, and extend the hand. Let's do all we can on our side of heaven to make community possible for those on the outside looking in. Let's be sure everyone in our sphere of influence gets the opportunity to hear Christ's claims and connect to his community. Let's be sure — always.

freedom from unsolvable problems

PUTTING THE TIGHTROPE TO WORK

As I (Bill) write this, a member of our small group is in Indiana. Last night, while his wife was traveling back to Illinois, she struck a stray truck tire on the highway. Thankfully — and miraculously — she is uninjured, though the van is in bad shape. He has had a rough couple of months, and his wife's accident was the last thing he needed right now. His life requires a lot of care, and he needs his friends more than ever.

Another member is facing an oppressive and sometimes abusive family history. He and his family are intentionally and courageously confronting the ghosts of the past, but the work is far from over. He needs to keep shining the light of truth on his heart and remain accountable to the group for the difficult but necessary process he has begun.

One brother has lost his father, moved, changed career paths twice, and fought a rigorous and bureaucracy-laden visa battle, trying to remain at work here in America. As leader of a new ministry venture, he needs to establish trust and rally people to a worthy cause. But amid these expectations, he needs a small community to walk with him and help his family establish roots in a new environment.

We recently had to confront another member about his intense pace of life yet match confrontation with love and kindness, not judgment and ridicule. Because of that loving confrontation, he has encouraged us all by being ruthlessly honest with himself about a character flaw—pride—and facing it head-on, determined to grow and change.

One group member is striving to incorporate transformational truth in every arena of life. He is one of the most intentional people I know when it comes to pursuing and obeying God's will. And he longs for relational intimacy with everyone in the group. But because we've added three new people to the group in the last few months, he faces the challenging prospect of not knowing everyone equally well.

Another man in our group is deeply rooted in the Word of God and is committed to speaking truth in areas of conflict and relational breakdown. He regularly invites accountability for his decisions and for quality relationships with his wife and children.

I love these men and their families. Each is walking a tightrope or two. Each faces one or more of the challenges we have described. And the group as a whole faces all six, and I must lead us to face these realities with hope, grace, truth, and joy. This is the stuff of real groups. This is the stuff of true community.

Is it really possible for a group to meet all six challenges and produce a thriving community? I believe it is possible, because I see it happening right before my eyes. Not perfectly. Not all the time. Not all six characteristics are prominently exhibited at every encounter in community or at every small group meeting. But awareness is half the game. Recognizing these challenges and embracing them with simple strategies can help a group make substantial progress into real group life, true community. One life at a time. One group at a time.

Taking It to the Church

Great things happen when groups begin to walk the small group tightrope. But even greater things happen when an entire church recognizes the potential and embraces the vision. As I (Russ) write this, I am still settling into my role as senior pastor of Meadowbrook Church, a job I commenced in August 2002. Although it is early in the process, groups across the church are beginning to grasp the implications of walking the tightrope.

When I started at Meadowbrook, I knew we had a great core of people who already embraced the small group value. Shortly after the church began in 1991, it set its sights on building a church of small groups. Ironically, my first connection with MbC, as we call it, was through periodic consultation designed to help them realize their small group vision.

But the previous five years had been difficult for the church, and the people were a little battle weary. A succession of challenges (a euphemism for painful ministry adversity) bombarded the church. The founding senior pastor and elders parted company, several staff members departed, and then a founding family left for another ministry. Dissension erupted, and the church soon withered to about half its peak attendance. These trials clouded the future and vision of a once-vibrant beacon in the difficult ministry territory of the northeastern United States. A courageous core of people held fast, though, believing God would answer prayers for fresh leadership.

I ended up being the answer—yet another testimony to the need to be careful what you ask for! Through a stunning but clear calling to MbC, Lynn and I embarked on yet another ministry adventure, helping and healing a wounded congregation. It's hard sometimes, but the rewards have been frequent and deeply satisfying—especially in the small group arena. We must recover lost momentum and rebuild fragmented areas. But from nearly the moment we arrived, a solid group of small group leaders leaned into the challenges and started gaining ground, one life, one group at a time.

These groups are putting on a tightrope-walking clinic, each group addressing one or more of the challenges we unpacked in earlier chapters. There is truth meeting life, a melding of care and discipleship, friends finding accountability, kindness bumping into confrontation, the first blooms of community made possible by tasks done together, and intimacy among people willing to open their hands and share the rich community they've discovered. Despite daunting challenges, true community is on the rise at Meadowbrook, largely because church leaders are willing to walk the tightrope. At the intersection of all these tensions, life-changing small groups are becoming the most often-visited side doors to our church.

This reality has come on us so quickly that as we planned a recent leadership retreat, we seized on a theme first created by Dave Treat, a Willow Creek staff member: "Think Small." We devoted an entire weekend to fueling our vision to build our church into what God is calling us to be—by infusing every part of our church life with community. To reinforce what we dream of becoming, we introduced a new set of small group values, which you'll readily recognize:

- *Spiritual transformation*—where truth meets life
- *Intentional shepherding*—by caring leaders
- *Authentic relationships*—built on mutual accountability
- *Healthy conflict*—to deepen relationships

- *Serving together*—done in community
- *Inclusive community*—as a means to intimacy

Before the retreat ended, we had cemented into our leadership core what I had already been observing: a church with leaders who had given themselves to walking the tightrope to true community.

I love these leaders and their groups. Each faces many other challenges in addition to those we have described. The church as a whole faces all six challenges. And I must lead us to face these realities with hope, grace, truth, and joy. This is the stuff of real church. This is the stuff of true community.

Is it really possible for a church to meet all six challenges and produce a thriving community in all its groups? I believe it is possible, because I see it happening right before my eyes. Not perfectly. Not all the time. The values we have presented don't automatically find life at all times. But seeing them as our future is half the game. Embracing these challenges and training leaders to take next steps can position them to take their groups into real group life, true community. One leader at a time. One church at a time.

A New Freedom

When groups and churches stop trying to solve unsolvable problems and instead enter into the tensions every ministry faces, authentic communities begin to form. And these communities begin to transform the culture of a church—one life, one leader, one group at a time. Instead of feeling guilty about not reaching unrealistic standards of performance, groups encounter the fresh winds of the Spirit blowing through their little community. Look again at the results.

- *Spiritual transformation*—people's lives are changing in conformity with truth.

- *Intentional shepherding*—caring leaders are moving people toward growth.
- *Authentic relationships*—friends care enough to challenge one another.
- *Healthy conflict*—problems are resolved and people are reconciled.
- *Serving together*—community is fostered while tasks are accomplished.
- *Inclusive community*—new people are enfolded into ever-deepening relationships.

When leaders understand that rigid group models and practices no longer bind them, they are indeed free. Free to fail, free to risk, free to become. Members will not be upset or surprised by confusion and clarity, grace and truth, chaos and control, laughter and tears—all in the same meeting!

But getting to all six results, without compromising the quality of your leadership, requires staring fearlessly into the reality of these tensions. So let's look again at the six challenges. Seeing them displayed all at once may overwhelm you, especially now that you've read and understood each challenge. But now you also know that these are realities in small group life and that each tension can find a healthy balance in a thriving community.

Challenge to Meet	Tightrope to Walk	Purpose to Achieve
Learning	Truth—Life	Spiritual Transformation
Development	Care—Discipleship	Intentional Shepherding
Relational	Friendship—Accountability	Authentic Relationships
Reconciliation	Kindness—Confrontation	Healthy Conflict
Impact	Task—People	Serving Together
Connection	Openness—Intimacy	Inclusive Community

A Look in the Mirror

Now that you have all six tensions in mind, we want you to bring together all the thinking from the previous chapters. It starts with honestly assessing your group. If you have read the chapters and have worked through the exercises in the appendix, you are ready to review your group's progress and opportunities. Using the chart above, ask yourself, "Where are we on each tightrope? How well are we meeting each challenge? Where do we tend to land on each tightrope? How well is our group accomplishing each purpose?" In the chart below, mark an *X* where you see your group on each continuum. Ask your group members for their opinions if you are doing this together.

Truth. . . . . Spiritual Transformation . . . . Life
Care . . . . Intentional Shepherding . . . . . Discipleship
Friendship . . . . . . Authentic Relationships . . . Accountability
Kindness. . . . . Healthy Conflict . . . . . . Confrontation
Task. . . . . Serving Together . . . . People
Openness . . . . Inclusive Community . . . . Intimacy

Once you have marked each continuum, it is time to determine next steps. What specific actions can your group take to help it embrace the tension by honoring both ends of each continuum? Which tightropes require the most attention? Seek help by reviewing prior chapters and what you determined as you worked through the appendix exercises.

Thoroughly answering these questions and choosing specific actions can be such a big job that you might not know where to start. So try shortening the time frame. Which area(s) needs the most attention over the next ninety days? Of the action steps you identified, what can most readily be pursued tomorrow? What will give the most return for the effort? How might you focus more energy on that area?

One additional step can really help — breaking down key goals into individual activities. Ask each group member to assess their contribution to the group's potential progress. While you may want to focus on specific tasks, you might benefit by moving from the specific to the more general chart of challenges, tightropes, and purposes. You might even want each group member to ask themselves, "Where is my heart on this issue? Where do I need to grow?"

When groups openly and honestly face the six challenges and walk the tightrope together, group life becomes an adventure. Meetings soon become moments of community; casual camaraderie gives way to true community. But this does not happen automatically. Mere discussion and understanding will not move a group forward. It will require your ongoing leadership. It always takes a leader, someone bold enough to walk the tightrope no matter what tensions may arise.

The Payoff for Small Group Tightrope Walking

Matt and Susan were leading a group of young couples like themselves in the Wheaton area, where Willow Creek was launching a regional campus. New people — especially young couples — were finding Christ through this new regional ministry, and small groups were needed to connect them and help them grow in Christ. At one group meeting, Matt and Susan shared their vision to open up their group and invite some of the new young couples who lived in the neighborhood. "Take a week to pray about how we might do that, and we will talk about it the next time we get together," they said.

The next meeting became a defining moment for the group. Only one couple was interested in opening the group to newcomers. The rest feared that the intimacy they had experienced would be destroyed. Matt and Susan faced a decision. Do we remain closed and invest in only the existing relationships, or do we follow our vision and open the group to some new people? It was a difficult decision, but they had to follow their vision for connecting the unconnected, a vision that fueled the entire regional ministry. They communicated their decision to open the group and, sadly, only one couple remained. The other members left.

It was an emotional time. Matt and Susan loved each group member and were discouraged that these friends couldn't embrace the vision and remain in the group. Nonetheless, the vision for openness had gripped these leaders. And they knew that, in reality, they shouldn't have to compromise relational intimacy in the process of reaching new people. So they began the new group, this time with a vision for creating a larger, safer environment to connect people. And before long, twenty to thirty new people were coming to the group. The openness vision was paying off. But now Matt and Susan feared that size and the constant influx of new people could jeopardize their ability to build deeply into these young couples.

The proverbial pendulum had swung the other way. It was time to focus on truth, discipleship, and intimacy in relationships. The leaders didn't want to stop connecting people, but they had to slow down the process and drive roots into the soil of this new community of thirty people. In effect, they were squarely on the tightrope, working with the tensions inherent in small group life.

Recognizing natural affinities within the new group, they decided to form two smaller groups—one for couples with children and one for those without. It seemed that relationships were forming along these lines anyway, so Susan and Matt made use of this dynamic. At a group retreat, they cast a new vision for starting the new groups. They clearly communicated the new vision for each group: *Do life, go deep, and draw in*. Practice doing life together, connecting regularly between meetings; build depth in relationships and foster discipleship; and draw others into the net. A powerful vision!

Soon there were three groups, each reaching out to young couples while building into the existing relationships. Susan and Matt continue to lead one group and provide direction and guidance to other leaders. Looking back over the four years it took them to get to this point, Matt and Susan are amazed at what God has done. First there was a single, closed group. Then it was reduced to a core of only four visionaries. Now there are three growing, vibrant, open groups. Wow! But it would not have happened without leaders who were willing to embrace the vision and follow God's leading. Matt and Susan courageously walked the openness-intimacy tightrope and met the connection challenge, fulfilling God's divine purpose for their little community.

Courageous Church Leadership

Christ called us not to control a community but simply to enter it. We have no mandate to control people like we manage systems, checking off little boxes and systematically handing out little flash cards. Why do we insist on making community a chore by subjecting people to mechanistic systems? Because we fear losing control. We need to feel like we've done our job at the end of the day.

You cannot define community. To define it is to limit it, to reduce it to a series of steps or components. Rather, community must be experienced because it is mysterious and broad and fluid. You can *describe* it. You can tell people what it looks like. But you cannot define it any more than you can define a painting by Rembrandt or Monet. The longer you look, the richer it becomes. To gaze on its beauty and revel in its mystery is to enjoy it fully. And in this way the painting's richness can be experienced time and again. Walk through the Rijksmuseum in Amsterdam and you will come upon Rembrandt's floor-to-ceiling painting *The Nightwatch*. Your stunned silence soon gives way to a wondrous awe, and you must find a seat and ponder this remarkable masterpiece, a work that cannot be digested in a single viewing. Go ahead, try to define it, if you must. But be duly warned. If you succeed, your experience will have ended abruptly. The artwork has been mastered, registered, catalogued — defined. There will be no need to ever return.

Though the tensions of the small group tightrope can be described on a chart, they cannot be solved by taking three simple steps or by following a paint-by-numbers approach to group life. The adventure and thrills come when a community enters the tunnel of chaos that is inherent in all authentic relational encounters. We must name our reality, express our needs and desires, and then courageously pursue becoming a true community. For the world to be influenced for Christ, people must see the real thing in action, not some plastic, inflexible impostor masquerading as the church. As one of our small group mentors, Gil Bilezikian, has said,

> In our day, whenever the church is ineffective in its witness and remains unproductive, the first questions that must be raised are whether the church functions as authentic community and whether

> it lives out the reality of its oneness. In a community-starved world, the most potent means of witness to the truth of the gospel is the magnetic power of the oneness that was committed by Christ to his new community at the center of history.[1]

The real thing cannot be easily ignored or readily dismissed. True community will be either loved or hated, just as Christ is. But people will know we are here. Lukewarm Christianity will become the exception, not the norm. Christ followers in little communities will declare the realities of the kingdom. Church leaders will trade the power to lead for the privilege to serve; ministry will not be done by a few but practiced by all; church will no longer be a place to go but rather a people to become; and groups will trade superficial connections for transforming community. And that's worth walking a few tightropes. So lace up your walking shoes.

LEADER'S GUIDE

and group interaction exercises

LEADER'S GUIDE FOR GROUP INTERACTION

The group exercises presented in this section are designed to help your group walk the small group tightrope together and meet each of the six challenges presented in this book. It is important for leaders to read each chapter before completing the corresponding exercise.

Ideally, each member will have a copy of the book so they can have an in-depth understanding of each tension, but if this isn't possible, leaders can provide a brief overview of the main points of the chapter to prepare the group for the exercise.

Each exercise is designed to maximize group participation and help members engage with the content of the chapter in ways that build community. Each group interaction includes instructions that provide the following:

Overview — a description of the meeting time including:

- Purpose
- Biblical information
- Time required
- Materials needed
- Activity to complete

Meeting Preparation — specific instructions to help group leaders guide their members in the exercise.

Walking the Tightrope — a group activity or interaction that will cause members to wrestle with the tension of each continuum we have discussed.

The exercises we will present focus on interactive, experiential learning and discussion. It may take more than one meeting to process the material for each of the six challenges, but it doesn't have to. You can set your own pace. We have included time guidelines to give you an idea of what an average group of eight to ten people might be able to accomplish during a meeting. We recognize your normal meeting will include other elements (such as a task, prayer, times for celebration and affirmation, Scripture reading, and so on).

We think you will enjoy processing what you have read. It will help your group begin to identify things they are already feeling and thinking and create an environment for group growth and personal transformation.

the learning challenge

CHAPTER 1

Overview

Purpose: To understand the role of truth in the life of the group and to explore how to integrate Scripture with life situations. Members will gain perspective on how truth must be applied, not simply understood.

Biblical Information: Hebrews 12:1–3; see also 1 Corinthians 9:24–26.

Time Required: 60 minutes preferred.

Materials Needed: Pens and paper for each member, index cards, and a Bible.

Activity to Complete: A group discussion in which you will attempt to bring truth and life together in a creative, practical way. Each member will be assigned a role associated with running a race. Using a familiar Scripture passage, help the group do two things: understand how sin and distractions can prevent a believer from running a good race, and creatively explore how to help each other finish the race well. The goal is to engage the group with the content of the passage (truth) and move them toward application (life), personally and as a community.

Meeting Preparation

Reading: Read chapter 1. Pay particular attention to the suggestions about how to turn a question into a discussion and how to vary learning styles. You will be using those skills in this exercise.

Scripture: Carefully read Hebrews 12:1–3 before coming to the meeting. This passage, familiar to many Christians, is particularly suited for a truth-life discussion. Here is some background to help you with the passage:

a. The "great cloud of witnesses" was just described in Hebrews 11. The Greek word for "witness" is similar to the English word "martyr" and describes one who testifies to the faith. Those who have gone before us, some having given their lives for the faith, are cheering us on.
b. Jesus is the author (starter) of the race, and he is at the finish line, having overcome opposition, suffering, and death. He has completed the race. Now he is helping us to run a good race.
c. The "race marked out for us" does not require our design. Christ has designed the race, having run it himself. It is the Christian life, and it is described in Scripture so we can live life with integrity and hope. The Bible is our guideline for running the race, and Jesus is our example and coach, so to speak. We can take courage when we suffer because he has led the way.
d. The "joy set before him [Christ]" was restored relationships — with the Trinity and with the new community, his church. On the cross, Christ was separated from both because of the sin he bore and the wrath he incurred on

our behalf. This made possible our redemption and our reconciliation with God and with each other. Christ's joy would be full after his resurrection, because he is reunited with the pure, loving fellowship of the Father and Spirit and with his bride, the church.

e. For the idea of perseverance in running the race, see also 1 Corinthians 9:24–26.

Materials: Write the following words on index cards. Put only one word on each card, making sure you use all the words. These are roles you will assign members of your group for the discussion. If you have less than five people, you might have to take more than one card for yourself.

- Coach
- Runner
- Judge
- Spectator (two or three cards can have this word on them)
- Enemy

Prayer: Pray for each member, asking God's Spirit to open their eyes to the truth and their hearts to obey it. Pray that your group members will courageously engage with the exercise.

Walking the Tightrope

Here is the group activity. Follow this process during the meeting.

Reading (2 minutes): Read Hebrews 12:1–3 together.

Questions to Ask the Group (10–15 minutes):

a. Who are the witnesses?

b. What are they doing?

c. What images come to mind when you compare the Christian life to a race?
d. Why is it important that Christ has already run the race?
e. What was Jesus' motivation and purpose for running the race?

Instructions for the Group (5 minutes): Hand out a card to each member of the group. Leaders should say something like this: "Look at your card. This is your perspective on the Christian race, your role for the next few minutes. Describe in a few words or phrases what you would be doing during the race." You can then present questions pertaining to each role to help members come up with ideas. For example,

- *Coach:* How might you prepare the runner for this race called the Christian life? What training would you require? What would you be doing while he or she was running?
- *Runner:* What challenges do runners face? What is going through your mind as you run? What can you do to stay focused on the finish line?
- *Judge:* How will you determine if a runner has run a good race? What would you like to say to the runner when the race is over?
- *Spectator:* What are you doing during the race? What are you saying to the runner?
- *Enemy:* Our main competitor is Satan. He doesn't seek to run the race and win but to make others stumble. List the sins that could take the runner out of the race. What temptations would you throw in his or her way?

Personal Work (5 minutes): Ask members to write their ideas on the card. Each person should think in terms of their assigned role.

Group Discussion (20–25 minutes): Ask each person to share aloud what they decided to do or say and have the other members respond. How does the coach feel about what the runner describes? What would the Judge (Christ) think? What does the enemy do or think when the spectators start cheering the runner on? Have some fun with this but try to uncover the root causes of sin and some strategies for meeting temptations and distractions at the personal level *and* as a group. How can we help one another run the race well?

Prayer (5–10 minutes): Break into groups of two or three. Have members briefly describe an obstacle that gets them tangled up, a stumbling block in their race. Is it a character flaw? A sin pattern? Uncontrolled anger? Ignoring the poor? Busyness? Then pray for one another, for strength, forgiveness, healing, and courage. Ask God's Spirit to act. And commit to support one another in the coming days and weeks.

the development challenge

CHAPTER 2

Overview

Purpose: To help groups understand the tension that exists when the expectations for care and discipleship meet each other head-on. Members will gain some perspective of the challenge a leader faces in guiding a group in the midst of this challenge and will become part of the solution. This will cause key discipleship issues to surface and help create care boundaries for groups when they are faced with problems similar to those in the case study that will be presented.

Biblical Information: Galatians 6:1–10.

Time Required: 45–60 minutes.

Materials Needed: One copy of the case study, presented below, for each member, unless everyone has this book.

Activity to Complete: The group will read the case study and attempt to wrestle with the tensions presented. Subgroups will be formed so that members can work together to address solutions and face the chaos created when care needs increase beyond normal levels.

Meeting Preparation

Reading: Read chapter 2. Be prepared to summarize key points for members who don't have the book. Also read through the case study.

Scripture: Read Galatians 6:1–10 and note the following:

a. The emphasis here is on carrying each other's moral burdens and weaknesses. We are to support one another when we sin and restore each other to the faith. We are all weak, and we all fail.
b. We are all responsible for our own load but also for helping others, knowing we reap what we sow. In the Greek text, two words for "burden" are used. One word denotes a lighter load, the other a heavy one. In effect, the passage says, "Carry one another's boulders, but each one should carry his own backpack."
c. We are to do good to all, especially to believers because we are a family and we should never neglect the family of God (1 Tim. 5:8).

Materials: Make copies of the case study for members who do not have the book.

Walking the Tightrope

Case Study (5 minutes): Read the following case study as a group.

A group at First Church has been meeting for nine months. Overall, solid relationships are being established, and several good studies have been completed using the church curriculum. The group has thirteen members, but usually no more than ten people are present at a meeting because of travel and other occasional schedule conflicts. It is a mixed group of men and women, some singles and some couples.

Members' ages range from twenty-three to fifty-seven, and all members live within five to ten minutes of each other. Sometimes younger children are included in meetings, especially when there is a meal and an extended gathering time.

For the last three months the group has been challenged by a demanding situation. Two months ago, Bob and Mary Peterson (average age fifty-three) were faced with taking Mary's mother into their home to provide care for her. She is in the early stages of Alzheimer's disease, and they want to keep her with them as long as possible, realizing the day will soon come when her needs will require full-time care in a facility.

Though Mary's mother is in the early stages of Alzheimer's, she requires attention and close watching. This has put a drain on Bob and Mary's marriage. Just two years ago, they had become "empty nesters," sending their last child off to college. They could finally focus more on their relationship, and they were enjoying the new opportunities facing them. But all that came to an abrupt end two months ago.

For the last eight meetings Bob and Mary have increasingly become the focus of the group. During times for prayer requests and sharing, sometimes twenty to thirty minutes is spent on the Petersons' situation. At first everyone was sensitive and understanding, but it is now starting to wear on the group. Other members feel they are getting slighted as more attention is paid to Bob and Mary.

Mary spends much group time talking about her mom, the needs she has, her frustrations, and so on. She requests prayer for her mother and has asked the group to help with some of the care needs (like meals, trips to the doctor's, taking care of the dog when they have to take her mother to an out-of-town facility for special testing and treatment). The group has been helpful and willing. But the needs are increasing, and the Petersons' are requiring more attention.

For four meetings now the group's Bible study time has been cancelled or dramatically shortened in light of this situation. Between meetings, members are doing their best to help Bob and Mary but now have less time to connect with each other. They are willing to help but are beginning to feel overwhelmed.

Bob has become increasingly honest with the group about his frustrations. He is five years from retirement, and his company is not doing well. He's hoping they won't fire him before he earns full pension. Other senior employees have been laid off to cut costs. Bob works hard and has a good relationship with his boss but is concerned that his position is in jeopardy. Now, on top of this, he has to spend his spare time caring for Mary's mom, running errands, and being available on weekends to help her.

He had hoped to spend more time with Mary and with his friends. He has had to give up his regular golf time every Saturday afternoon, and he and Mary can't go on walks like they used to because her mom cannot be left alone for very long. He is angry and tired, and it is beginning to cause a rift in their relationship.

For the first six to seven months of the Petersons' extra care needs, the small group leaders, Kevin and Dana (average age thirty-two, with two small children), have been following the growth plan and curriculum recommended by the church, the one all leaders use with adult groups. It contains a series of Scripture readings, study questions, and discipleship initiatives. The group has been memorizing two Scriptures each month and is maturing in personal and group prayer. Monthly, many members gather on a Saturday morning to serve at the Brotherhood Mission in the city, where they clean the facility for the homeless men who stay there. Members have been challenged to grow in their understanding of the Word and to look at areas for growth. Discussions on these issues have been lively and engaging.

There have been other care challenges in the group (Steve's five-day bout with a devastating flu virus, the death of Lisa's father five months ago in an auto accident, and the burglary at the Blakes' home this past winter). But most of these situations required a temporary response, and the group became a great source of strength and support for these members in need. But the Petersons' situation looks like a long-term challenge.

Group frustration is mounting, the Petersons are weak and wounded, members are longing for the group dynamic that was being experienced several months ago, and the group leaders rarely accomplish 30 percent of what they plan for a meeting. During the last two months, only three of the required six people showed up to serve at the mission, and the director is wondering if he can count on the group's help. The Petersons have had to stop serving there, and other members often find themselves helping Mary when Bob's travels take him out of town for a weekend. For many members, the only time to get personal chores done before kids' activities begin is Saturday mornings, let alone serve at the mission and help the Petersons.

Subgroup Work (10 minutes): After reading the case study, break the group into three smaller groups, A, B, and C. Group A should focus on the care needs of the members in the case study, including the Petersons. Group B should focus on the need for the group to grow spiritually and on the overall direction of the group. Group C will look at the role of the leaders. (Note: You as group leader should participate in group A or B, not group C.)

Questions for Subgroups to Consider:

Group A

How should the group respond to the Petersons' situation?

What care can be given to the Petersons during meetings?

What can be done for them between meetings?

How can the needs of the other members be addressed?

What boundaries can be drawn for meetings and for the time between meetings?

How should the church staff be involved, if at all?

Group B

What can be done to refocus the group on spiritual-growth issues?

How can this be done without dishonoring the Petersons?

What can members expect on a regular basis when it comes to Scripture, prayer, and growth?

What role should the group's curriculum play during this time?

Group C

What attitudes should the leaders model and expect the group to embrace?

How can the leaders set boundaries?

When and how should they talk to the Petersons?

What adjustments can they make in the group process? During meetings? Between meetings?

Debriefing (15–20 minutes): Now ask each subgroup to give their best feedback and suggestions. Allow other members to respond.

Scripture and Response (10 minutes): Read Galatians 6:1–10 aloud and have the group respond to the following questions:

How do we carry our own burdens, and when is it time to help carry one another's burdens?

How do we exhort one another not to grow weary in "doing good," even if it is hard?

Prayer (5–10 minutes): Pray for wisdom and discernment for one another, and especially for the small group leaders. Ask members to pray for you, the leader, because this is a difficult tightrope for you to walk.

the relational challenge

CHAPTER 3

Overview

Purpose: To help people define the relational environment of the group and understand the expectations of each member regarding this environment.

Biblical Information: Passages from Proverbs, listed below.

Time Required: 45 minutes minimum; 60 minutes or more preferred.

Materials Needed: Pens, paper, and scissors for each member, some old magazines that have plenty of photos of people in real life (news magazines, magazines that focus on people and events, possibly some sports magazines).

Activity to Complete: Group assessment and interaction. The goal is to provoke self-disclosure and allow members to respond with affirmation, support, acceptance, and truth telling.

Meeting Preparation

Read: Read chapter 3. Pay particular attention to the information about knowing, loving, serving, admonishing, and celebrating.

Scripture: Read the wisdom of Proverbs 12:26; 16:28; 17:17; 18:24; 19:4, 6; 22:11, 24; 27:6, 9, 10. Friendships are fragile. The teaching in these verses is quite plain about the risks and rewards of close relationships.

Materials: Gather some magazines from which members can cut photos of people. You will also need scissors for each member and paper for people to jot down their thoughts.

Walking the Tightrope

Assessment (10 minutes): Ask members to rate the group in each area discussed in chapter 3. How would they say the group is doing in each of the following areas?

1 = weak   3 = average   5 = strong

Know and Be Known	1	2	3	4	5
Love and Be Loved	1	2	3	4	5
Serve and Be Served	1	2	3	4	5
Admonish and Be Admonished	1	2	3	4	5
Celebrate and Be Celebrated	1	2	3	4	5

Take a few minutes to discuss why people rated the group as they did and in which area they think the group needs the most improvement.

Magazines (5 minutes): Now let's look at what you can do to help the group develop in these areas and build authentic relationships. Grab a magazine and find two photos, one that evokes feelings of laughter or joy, and one that evokes thoughts of an area for character growth or change. Jot down a few words as to why these photos move you the way they do.

Self-Disclosure and Response (15–20 minutes): Members should briefly discuss why they chose the photos they did (1–2 minutes). One or two other members can ask questions of clarification about the comments made. After each member has shared, you may take the discussion deeper, but make sure each person gets a turn to explain their photos. So watch your time. (You may want to have everyone explain the photos first, then come back and start the discussion. Or if you feel this discussion needs more time and members are really interacting well, you may want to carry it over to another meeting. You could even spend an extended time together around a meal and really engage with this exercise!)

Encourage members to practice acceptance, provide affirmation, and offer support to one another as people describe the photos they chose. Also listen carefully to members as they share about character growth; you may get some ideas for developing or increasing mutual accountability. Encourage truth telling and honest interaction. This exercise may uncover some hidden joys or deep concerns among members, and this is a great time to create a safe and encouraging environment in the group.

Scripture and Prayer (10 minutes): Read some of the Proverbs aloud and tell the group that you want to build relationships even though they are fragile at times and take work. Then spend a few moments in prayer as a group.

the reconciliation challenge

CHAPTER 4

Overview

Purpose: To help the group enter into the process of healthy conflict management. The goal is to get a clear biblical picture of healthy conflict, identify personal sticking points, and encourage next steps toward reconciliation with people in members' lives.

Biblical Information: Matthew 5:23–24; 18:15–18; Ephesians 4:17–5:2

Time Required: 45–60 minutes.

Materials Needed: Pens and paper for each member and a Bible.

Activity to Complete: Bible study, self-assessment, and teamwork.

Meeting Preparation

Reading: Read chapter 4 and review the root causes of conflict, and read the appendix, "Navigating Breakdown." Also recognize that people tend to focus on either kindness or confrontation. How would you describe each member in your group along the kindness-confrontation continuum?

Scripture: Look at Matthew 5:23–24; 18:15–18; and Ephesians 4:17–5:2, noting the comments about speaking the truth in love to one another. You don't need to focus on all of these passages in the meeting, but you may need to refer to some of this material as questions or comments arise. Here are some of the insights from these passages:

a. You must initiate conflict resolution.
b. Worship is compromised when relational sin exists.
c. Do not let your hearts become hardened.
d. Put off the old self and live as Christ did, aligning with the truth.
e. Express anger, but do not sin in word or deed while doing so.
f. The devil will always seek to use conflict to destroy community.
g. Serve and give to others, becoming less selfish.
h. Use words to build up, not tear down.
i. Relational breakdown grieves the Holy Spirit.
j. Trade bitterness and rage for kindness, compassion, and forgiveness.
k. Model a life of love and service to others.

Prayer: This exercise will encourage people to become open about their own conflict avoidance. There are many reasons conflict may arise (as mentioned in chapter 4), but you want to focus on why people are afraid to enter into the process of confronting conflict. Pray about the meeting and that the Lord would soften the heart of each member.

Walking the Tightrope

Subgroup Work: Divide the group into two smaller groups, A and B.

Scripture Study (15 minutes): Ask members to read Ephesians 4:17–5:2.

Ask Group A to write down all of the positive consequences of obeying what is taught in this passage about conflict in relationships. What character qualities are necessary for believers to handle conflict well?

Ask Group B to write down the consequences of ignoring the guidelines mentioned in the passage. What kinds of behavior or attitudes prevail in people that cause conflict and destroy relationships?

Debriefing (10 minutes): Give each group five minutes to present what they discovered in the passage.

Personal Work (5 minutes): Now comes the hard part. Ask group members to picture someone with whom they have unresolved conflict or a relational fracture that has been avoided. Maybe it is a spouse, or family member, an acquaintance at work, or someone in the small group. Have members write the person's name down and ask them to list the steps they would need to take to begin the process of reconciliation. Also ask them to consider whether they are a "kindness" person or a "confrontation" person. This will affect how they approach people when there is a relational breakdown.

You may want to prompt them by asking, "Is your next step a personal meeting, a look at your heart, prayer, writing down your feelings in a journal, Scripture study and reflection, or asking God to change your attitude?

Prayer and Encouragement (10 minutes): Have members pair up with someone else in the group and describe why it has been hard to enter the reconciliation challenge. Ask them to avoid sharing the details of what they wrote down — that is gossip — and instead focus on areas where they need prayer so that they can begin the reconciliation process. If a member has an unreconciled problem with another member, this may be an ideal time for them to sit down and begin to offer confession and extend forgiveness. Members should encourage one another and pray for strength and courage to initiate reconciliation.

Group Time (10 minutes): Debrief on what has happened and discuss some ways the group can become a safe place to handle or address conflicts that may arise within the group.

the impact challenge

CHAPTER 5

Overview

Purpose: To help community-focused groups consider their responsibilities and opportunities to serve, and to help serving-oriented groups to build deeper relationships.

Biblical Information: Romans 16:1–16; Philippians 2:1–4.

Time Required: 30–40 minutes.

Materials Needed: Pens and paper for each member.

Activity to Complete: Brainstorming and planning an activity together.

Meeting Preparation

Reading: Read chapter 5. Be prepared to explain the main ideas to group members who do not have the book.

Scripture: Romans 16:1–16 and Philippians 2:1–4.

Research: If you lead a task group or a serving team, review your calendar to see when members might be available for a special group outing or community-building time together. If you lead a community-focused group, ask church leaders about opportunities for your group to serve together.

Walking the Tightrope

For Community Groups

Scripture (10 minutes): Read Romans 16:1–16; Philippians 2:1–4. Discuss the quality and nature of Paul's relationships. How did serving alongside others contribute to the depth of Paul's friendships? What motivated Christ to serve others?

Brainstorming (10 minutes): Describe to members how serving together can help your group deepen existing relationships and form new ones. Have the group brainstorm on how you can meet the needs of people outside your group.

Planning (15 minutes): Choose a time, place, and serving activity you can do together and put it on the calendar. Determine what preparations are necessary to accomplish the task and assign roles and responsibilities.

Close with Prayer

For Serving Groups

Scripture (10 minutes): Read Philippians 2:1–4. What attitudes should accompany serving? What motives should be in place? How can these be developed on your team? Look at the list in Romans 16:1–16. Paul didn't simply complete a task; he built relationships with people. How did this affect his ministry?

Brainstorming (10 minutes): Have members brainstorm on how you can deepen the relational nature of your task group or serving team. What can be done during the serving time, before or after the serving time, and throughout the week? What special gatherings can be created to deepen community?

Planning (15 minutes): Determine a date for a miniretreat or a time for an extended meal and fellowship. Consider including members' families. Determine a time and location and assign responsibilities for preparations. What kind of event will you hold? What relationship-building activities or exercises will you include? (If you need help here, *Leading Life-Changing Small Groups* has several pages of such activities you might want to consider.) How often should you hold a gathering like this?

Close with Prayer

the connection challenge

CHAPTER 6

Overview

Purpose: To help people acknowledge the risks involved in inviting newcomers into the group as well as the risks involved in deepening the intimacy of the group.

Biblical Information: Acts 2:42–47.

Time Required: 45 minutes.

Materials Needed: Bibles, two large sheets of poster board or large sheets of paper (at least 20 x 20 inches), markers for each member.

Activity to Complete: Personal stories and reflections, assessment, and determining next steps to take as a group.

Meeting Preparation

Reading: Read chapter 6.

Scripture: Read Acts 2:42–47 and note how intimacy and depth of true community naturally lead to the adding of new members. Notice how the interactions within the body were so compelling that others were drawn by God to enter in. When a community is truly growing, it welcomes with open arms people outside the community.

Materials: On the top of your paper or poster board, write the equation presented in chapter 6 as follows:

Sheet 1: Love + Gratitude + Risk = Openness

Sheet 2: Duration + Confidentiality + Risk = Intimacy

Walking the Tightrope

Stories (5 minutes): Look at the equation on sheet 1: Love + Gratitude + Risk = Openness. Ask members when they were first connected to a group of believers. Have them briefly list words or phrases that capture what it felt like. Then have someone write these words and phrases under the equation on the poster board so that everyone can see the responses.

Questions for the Group (10 minutes): What risks are associated with opening this small group to newcomers? How might we address those risks? What benefits might we experience by opening our group? How might we actually deepen intimacy by adding new people? What might lost people experience when they enter a community of loving believers?

Stories (5 minutes): Look at the equation on sheet 2: Duration + Confidentiality + Risk = Intimacy. Have members describe in a few words or phrases the qualities of their closest, most intimate relationships. Then ask someone to write members' responses on the poster board under the equation.

Questions for the Group (10 minutes): Describe the risks you took to create intimacy in your marriage or in a close relationship. Why was this hard? What did you fear?

Reality Check (15 minutes): Put the poster boards side by side, and review what is written under each equation. Consider the following characteristics that were presented in chapter 6 concerning the dynamics of openness:

a. The temptation to hoard community
b. The tendency for relationships to stagnate
c. The reality of mobility in our culture
d. The opportunity for natural relationships in our neighborhoods and workplaces
e. The opportunity to leave a legacy in the lives of others

In light of what is written on the poster boards, discuss which of the dynamics most likely impacts your group in ways that affect the extent of your group's openness. Can you honor the value of intimacy and still add some people to your little community?

Scripture and Questions (10 minutes): Read Acts 2:42–47. What would it take for us to build the level of openness and intimacy that the early community worked to build? How is openness a natural result of true community?

Prayer (10 minutes): Pray that God will open your hearts to extending community so that people can experience the intimacy you long for. Pray for wisdom concerning how to do this as a group.

navigating breakdown

The following guidelines apply whether you are navigating conflict between members or as an entire group. You may need to put on the vice principal hat and speak some hard truth. Or perhaps it's time for a "heart-to-heart" with a brother or sister who rubs you the wrong way.*

Guideline 1: Start Soon

You may need space to settle your emotions, but don't put off conflict for two weeks. Reconcile as soon as you can. I (Bill) remember an emotional conversation with a staff member in another church. The discussion remained biblical but started to heat up. My frustrated colleague said, "Well, nine months ago you offended me when you said . . ." Nine months ago! I wondered what other offenses he had filed away. Frankly, for nine months I felt fine. But he let this offense eat at his soul for nine months rather than bring it up with me.

Guideline 2: Meet Face to Face

Not e-mail! A Willow Creek leader received a stinging e-mail from a man in his small group. Instead of phoning for an appointment, the

---

*This appendix is taken from Bill Donahue and Russ Robinson, *Building a Church of Small Groups* (Grand Rapids: Zondervan, 2001), 97–98.

leader fired back a zinger. After several electronic exchanges, he realized: "Uh-oh, I shouldn't have done the e-mail thing." This was the understatement of the week. He is a good leader but let his emotions get the best of him. Their online communication created a permanent record of words but robbed them of the chance to read emotions, faces, and tone of voice. Snail mail has the same drawbacks.

Guideline 3: Affirm the Relationship

Remind people that you are trying to resolve this conflict precisely because you care about them and about your relationship. The way Russ confronted me about performance affirmed that he wanted to build on what we had. Now, years after that confrontation, here we are writing a book together. Because we sought to work it through biblically, we have a deepening friendship and close working relationship.

Guideline 4: Make Observations, Not Accusations

It's one thing to say, "Now, Bob, I've asked for that report three times and each time you promised that you would give it to me 'the next day.' As I understand the situation, this is a broken promise and a lack of commitment to the work we need to get done. It is unacceptable. I feel that you do not respect my authority, and we need to resolve this immediately." It's another thing to blurt out, "Bob, you're a liar! Three times you told me you would do this and you haven't. You're a liar!" The first approach is firm and direct but involves making observations about what is seen, heard, felt, and understood. The second approach is an accusation. Calling Bob a liar is a character assassination. It puts character in question and places him on the defensive.

Guideline 5: Get the Facts

Besides offering your own observations, be sure to let the other person respond. You might say, "Here's what I saw, heard, and felt; now, what did *you* see? What do *you* understand about this situation? Am I missing something?"

Guideline 6: Promote Resolution

The point of navigating conflict is not to fight, win, or prove who's more holy; it is to restore relationships we value. We want to reach consensus and move forward. Sometimes that may mean agreeing to disagree or deciding to overlook an offense for the sake of the relationship. In either case, we agree not to resurrect the offense. We decide together what next steps, if any, must be taken on the road to resolution—and we abide by them. Trust has been broken. Sticking to the arrangement will rebuild some of that trust.

notes

Introduction

1. Bill Donahue and the Willow Creek Small Groups Team, *Leading Life-Changing Small Groups,* rev. ed. (Grand Rapids: Zondervan, 1996, 2002).
2. Barry Johnson, *Polarity Management: Identifying and Managing Unsolvable Problems* (Amherst, Mass: HRD Press, 1992, 1996). Polarity Management™ is a trademark of Polarity Management Associates, LLC.

Chapter 1

1. Parker Palmer, *To Know as We Are Known* (San Francisco: HarperSanFrancisco, 1993), 23.
2. Fareed Zakaria, "The Character of Our Campuses," *Newsweek,* 28 May 2001, 31.
3. LaTonya Taylor, "The Church of O," *Christianity Today,* 1 April 2002, 39.
4. Palmer, *To Know as We Are Known,* 48–49.

Chapter 2

1. Sheryl Fleisher, Masters Internship Director at Willow Creek Community Church, developed this course and the core concepts we outline for intentional shepherding. For more information and audiotapes regarding this training course, please visit the Willow Creek Association web site at www.willowcreek.com, or call a WCA customer service representative at 847-765-0070.

Chapter 3

1. John Shaughnessy, "Lack Close Friends? Refrigerator Is Clue," *Courier Journal* (Louisville, Ky.), 2 December 2002.
2. Ibid.
3. Bill Donahue and Russ Robinson, *Building a Church of Small Groups* (Grand Rapids: Zondervan, 2001), 60–70.

Chapter 4

1. We have taught this often and have also been inspired and enlightened by the insightful teaching of Dr. Gilbert Bilezikian and John Ortberg in conferences at Willow Creek over the years.
2. Gilbert Bilezikian, *Community 101* (Grand Rapids: Zondervan, 1997), 37.
3. This is another topic on which we have previously provided teaching. For more principles on healthy conflict resolution, see Donahue and Robinson, *Building a Church of Small Groups,* 89–103.
4. Jean Vanier, *Community and Growth* (Mahwah, N.J.: Paulist, 1999), 37–38.

Chapter 5

1. Gallup Organization News Service, Poll Analyses, (Gallup Poll conducted December 9–10, 2002, for CNN/*USA Today),* 24 December 2002, by David W. Moore.
2. Ibid.
3. Lyle E. Schaller, *Leadership Journal* 17, no. 1 (winter 1986): 95–96.
4. See Bill Donahue and Russ Robinson, "Sin Six: Narrow Definition of a Small Group," chapter 11 in *The Seven Deadly Sins of Small Group Ministry* (Grand Rapids: Zondervan, 2002), 153–65.

Chapter 6

1. Tony Campolo, *The Kingdom of God Is a Party* (Dallas: Word, 1992), 4–9.
2. For more about apprentice development, see Donahue, *Leading Life-Changing Small Groups*, 67–76.
3. Vanier, *Community and Growth,* 267.
4. Ibid., 26–27.
5. For more on covenants, see Donahue, *Leading Life-Changing Small Groups*, 87–89.
6. Brenda Benner, *Texas National Guard Magazine,* June 2001, 6–8.

Conclusion

1. Bilezikian, *Community 101,* 37.

Willow Creek Association

Vision, Training, Resources for Prevailing Churches

This resource was created to serve you and to help you build a local church that prevails. It is just one of many ministry tools that are part of the Willow Creek Resources® line, published by the Willow Creek Association together with Zondervan.

The Willow Creek Association (WCA) was created in 1992 to serve a rapidly growing number of churches from across the denominational spectrum that are committed to helping unchurched people become fully devoted followers of Christ. Membership in the WCA now numbers over 10,000 Member Churches worldwide from more than ninety denominations.

The Willow Creek Association links like-minded Christian leaders with each other and with strategic vision, training, and resources in order to help them build prevailing churches designed to reach their redemptive potential. Here are some of the ways the WCA does that.

- **Prevailing Church Conference**—an annual two-and-a-half day event, held at Willow Creek Community Church in South Barrington, Illinois, to help pioneering church leaders raise up a volunteer core while discovering new and innovative ways to build prevailing churches that reach unchurched people.
- **Leadership Summit**—a once-a-year, two-and-a-half-day conference to envision and equip Christians with leadership gifts and responsibilities. Presented live at Willow Creek as well as via satellite broadcast to over sixty locations across North America, this event is designed to increase the leadership effectiveness of pastors, ministry staff, volunteer church leaders, and Christians in the marketplace.
- **Ministry-Specific Conferences**—throughout each year the WCA hosts a variety of conferences and training events—both at Willow Creek's main campus and offsite, across the U.S. and around the world—targeting church leaders in ministry-specific areas such as: evangelism, the arts, children, students, small groups, preaching and teaching, spiritual formation, spiritual gifts, raising up resources, etc.

- **Willow Creek Resources®**—to provide churches with trusted and field-tested ministry resources in such areas as leadership, evangelism, spiritual formation, spiritual gifts, small groups, stewardship, student ministry, children's ministry, the use of the arts—drama, media, contemporary music—and more. For additional information about Willow Creek Resources® call the Customer Service Center at 800-570-9812. Outside the U.S. call 847-765-0070.
- ***WillowNet***—the WCA's Internet resource service, which provides access to hundreds of transcripts of Willow Creek messages, drama scripts, songs, videos, and multimedia tools. The system allows users to sort through these elements and download them for a fee. Visit us online at www.willowcreek.com.
- ***WCA News***—a quarterly publication to inform you of the latest trends, resources, and information on WCA events from around the world.
- ***Defining Moments***—a monthly audio journal for church leaders featuring Bill Hybels and other Christian leaders discussing probing issues to help you discover biblical principles and transferable strategies to maximize your church's redemptive potential.
- ***The Exchange***—our online classified ads service to assist churches in recruiting key staff for ministry positions.
- **Member Benefits**—includes substantial discounts to WCA training events, a 20 percent discount on all Willow Creek Resources®, access to a Members-Only section on WillowNet, monthly communications, and more. Member Churches also receive special discounts and premier services through WCA's growing number of ministry partners—Select Service Providers.

For specific information about WCA membership, upcoming conferences, and other ministry services contact:

Willow Creek Association

P.O. Box 3188, Barrington, IL 60011-3188

Phone: 847-570-9812

Fax: 847-765-5046

www.willowcreek.com

We want to hear from you. Please send your comments about this book to us in care of zreview@zondervan.com. Thank you.

GRAND RAPIDS, MICHIGAN 49530 USA

WWW.ZONDERVAN.COM